ARB
4X4 ACCESSORIES

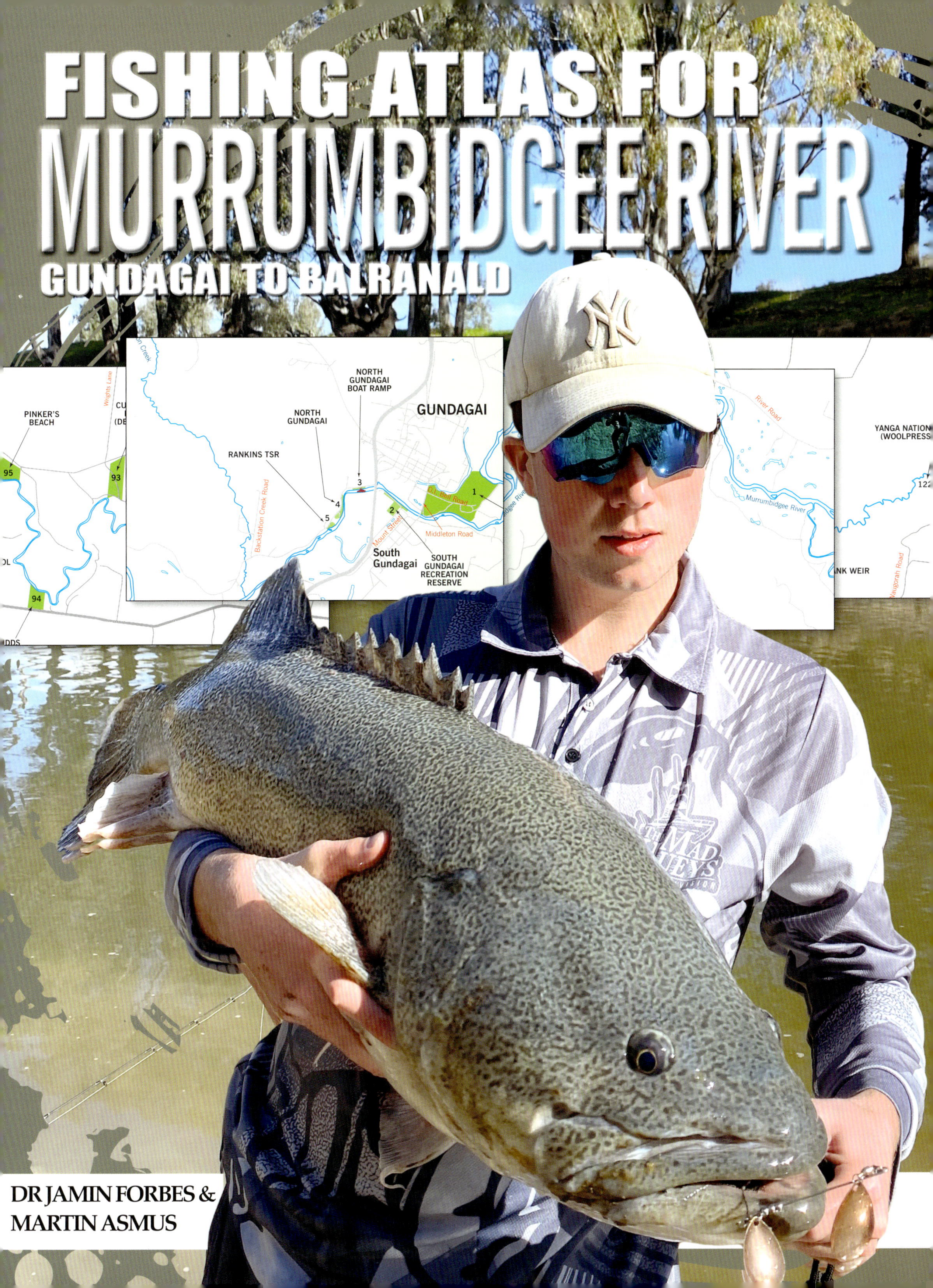
FISHING ATLAS FOR
MURRUMBIDGEE RIVER
GUNDAGAI TO BALRANALD
PINKER'S BEACH
95
93
94
Wrights Lane
NORTH GUNDAGAI BOAT RAMP
GUNDAGAI
NORTH GUNDAGAI
RANKINS TSR
Backstation Creek Road
1
2
3
4
5
Middleton Road
Mount Street
South Gundagai
SOUTH GUNDAGAI RECREATION RESERVE
River Road
Murrumbidgee River
DR JAMIN FORBES &
MARTIN ASMUS

Front cover: Tully Forbes cradling a trophy-sized Murray cod prior to release.

First published 2021

Published and distributed by
Australian Fishing Network
PO Box 544, Croydon, Victoria 3136
Telephone: (03) 9729 8788 Facsimile: (03) 9729 7833
Email: sales@afn.com.au
Website: www.afn.com.au

ISBN: 9781865133 843

CONTENTS

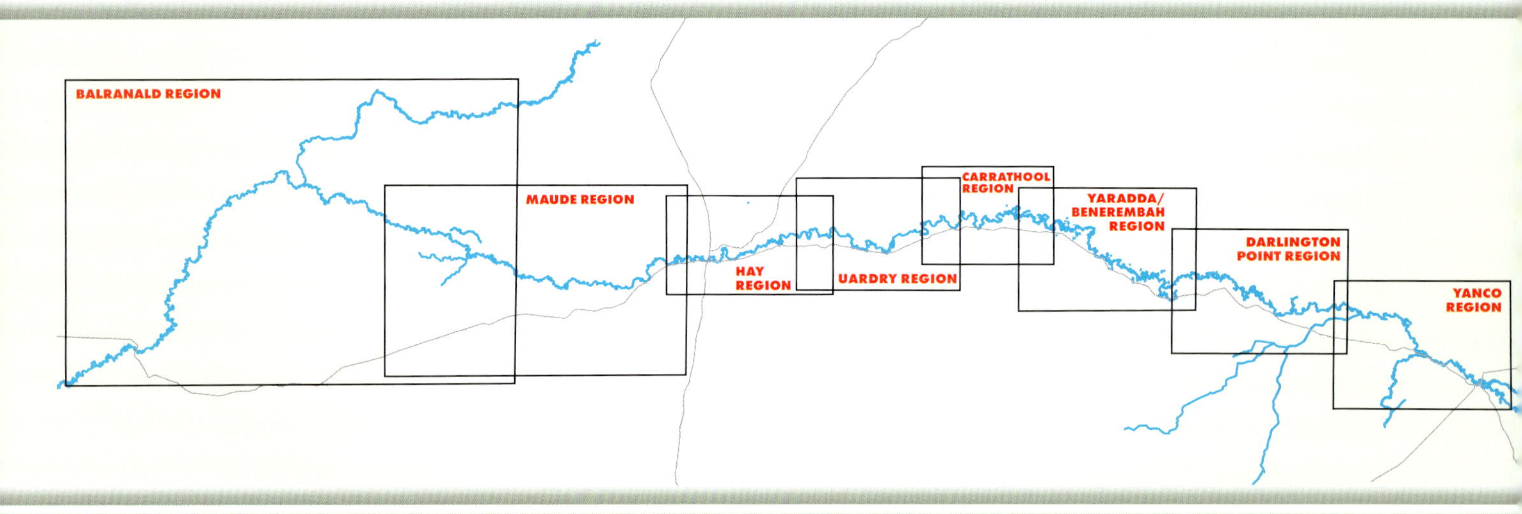
BALRANALD REGION
MAUDE REGION
HAY REGION
UARDRY REGION
CARRATHOOL REGION
YARADDA/ BENEREMBAH REGION
DARLINGTON POINT REGION
YANCO REGION

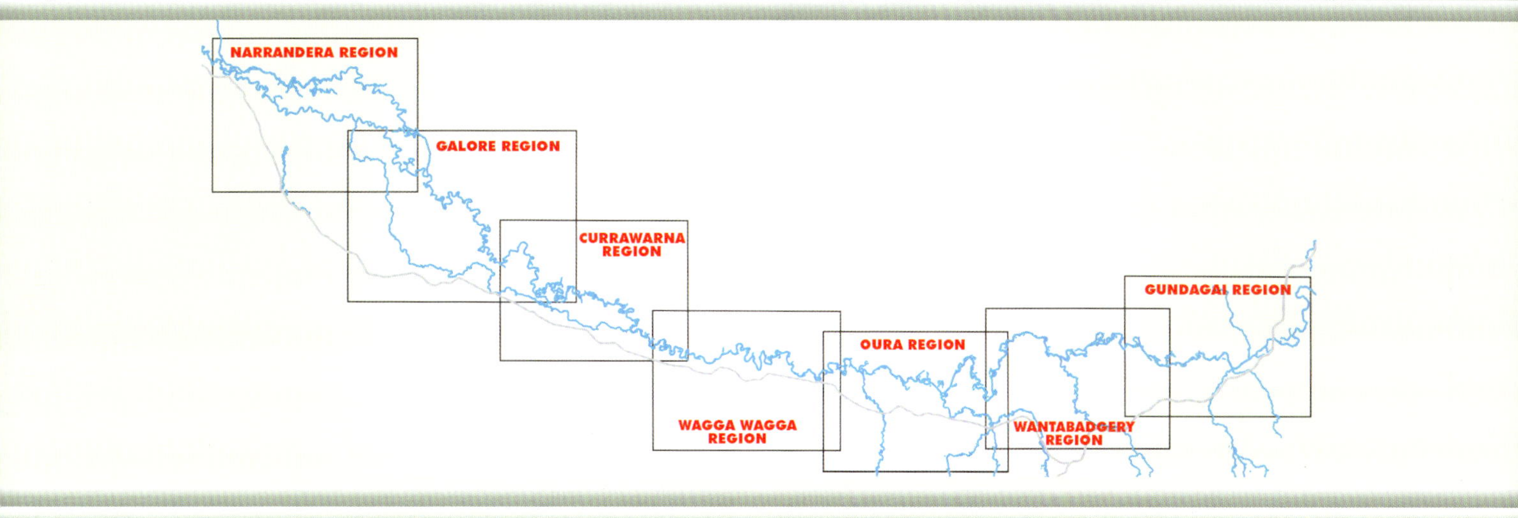
NARRANDERA REGION
GALORE REGION
CURRAWARNA REGION
GUNDAGAI REGION
OURA REGION
WAGGA WAGGA REGION
WANTABADGERY REGION

INTRODUCTION

The Murrumbidgee River has its headwaters in the Snowy Mountains, generally winding in a westerly direction for 1,485 km through the regional centres of Gundagai, Wagga Wagga, Narrandera, Hay and Balranald until it meets the Murray River near Boundary Bend.

The river parallels the Sturt Highway, which was named after the explorer Charles Sturt. On 3 November 1829, Charles Sturt departed Sydney to determine the course of the Murrumbidgee River. His expedition started near Jugiong and commenced overland before Sturt's famous whaleboat was launched on 7 January 1830, near the present township of Maude. A week later, Sturt exited the Murrumbidgee River into a new waterway which he termed 'a broad and noble river' — the river we now call the Murray.

In modern times, the Murrumbidgee River provides water for agricultural, domestic and industrial use and is the lifeblood on which the Riverina and surrounding regions depend. The topography surrounding the Murrumbidgee River changes markedly along its length. From Gundagai located at the foot of the Snowy Mountains, through the City of Wagga Wagga, to the irrigation hubs of Narrandera and Leeton, the vast treeless plain at Hay to the edge of the Mallee at Balranald. Through these areas, the Murrumbidgee River can be publicly accessed in over 130 locations.

This guide shows where these access points are and what you can expect to find on arrival. A series of maps, pictures, GPS co-ordinates and a commentary for each area will assist you to enjoy the Murrumbidgee River.

DISCLAIMER

While every care is taken to ensure accuracy of the information presented, the authors do not guarantee accuracy, reliability, completeness or suitability for any particular purpose. The authors define 'camping' and derivatives of this term, to jointly refer to day use and multi-day camping. Regulations exist that exclude overnight stays in some areas. Prospective campers must abide by local regulations and are advised to contact the relevant authority. The authors disclaim all responsibility and liability for any expenses, losses, damages (including indirect or consequential damages) and costs which may be incurred from the information presented in this book.

HOW TO USE THIS BOOK

Central to using this guide is interpreting the descriptions. Each site has a 'star' rating from one (poor) to five (excellent) for a range of physical attributes. The site-specific comments provide additional detail and highlight important features.

ACCESS ROADS: A five star access road is bitumen. A one star road is suitable for 4WD only. With the exception of wet weather, a three star road is 2WD accessible, but may be rough.

BOAT RAMP: 5 star boat ramps are 2WD accessible concrete. Four stars is 2WD accessible dirt, stone or gravel ramp, whilst three stars refer to a dirt ramp that is generally a sloping bank. Anything less than three stars is a difficult place to launch a trailer boat.

CAMPING: A rating below three stars is a poor camping area because of limited space, uneven ground, dense foliage, or a lack of shade. A four or five star campsite is generally characterised by flat ground, good shade, generally short grass and river access. Note that 'camping' jointly refers to day-use and multi-day use.

SWIMMING: Four or five star swimming sites are usually gently sloping, shallow beaches with slow moving current. Lesser rated swimming areas are often restricted by fast current, deep mud or steep banks. A single star rating suggests that it's possible to swim, but isn't recommended.

SHORE BASED FISHING: A five star angling bank provides excellent fish habitat, such as a drop-off, large eddies, deep water and/or submerged snags. Ratings less than three stars indicate that the foreshore access is restricted or the water may be shallow.

TOILETS: The presence or absence of toilets is usually indicated by at least one star, however a single star toilet is generally a 'pit' style toilet that is rarely serviced. A five star toilet is a serviced, clean facility.

SHADE: Dense shade provided by large trees such as river red gums or silky oaks receive five stars. Isolated trees with sparse foliage are rated as three stars. One star shade is minimal and usually limited to specific times of day, which exposes camps to full sun at some stage.

BINS: Bins are generally only provided on major reserves in urban areas. Reserve users should remove all rubbish and not contribute to illegal dumping.

BARBEQUES: The presence of a four or five star rating for barbeques indicates an electric or gas facility. A five star rating will have an associated shade structure and benches with the barbeque. Three stars or less indicates a fireplace with a barbeque plate in varying states of repair.

TABLE/BENCH: High quality timber or metal tables and associated benches with a shade structure receive five stars. Three stars are given to a table/bench in fair condition, whilst a damaged or badly deteriorated table or bench receives a single star.

CHAPTER 1
FISHING THE MURRUMBIDGEE

Fishing the Murrumbidgee River is separated into two methods – bait and lures. Both methods are effective at catching fish, however at certain times and conditions either technique can be more productive.

For example, when the river is high and turbid, bait fishing is usually more effective. However, when the river is low and clear, lure fishing is very effective. In winter, when water temperatures are at or below ten degrees, it can be difficult to catch a fish at all, with the exception of large Murray cod that remain active through the colder months (though it can be a long wait between bites). Murray crayfish are active in winter and provide an option when other species are less active (in areas where crayfishing is permitted).

In the warmer months when fish and fisherman are most active, it's the anglers' preference as to which method they use. Bait fishing will attract more bites (particularly from small fish), which suits a family fishing day, whereas lure fishing is an active pursuit involving a higher degree of skill. Lure fishing has the advantage of generally attracting larger fish, but fewer in number.

CHAPTER 2
BAIT FISHING

Effective bait fishing requires significant effort. To achieve regular catches, angling should not be a sedentary process (though waiting for a bite can be relaxing). Constant location changes find hungry fish.

Boat fishers should choose locations with plenty of snags. The boat should be positioned upstream (within casting range) of any structure. Cast your baits just in front of structure and/or along current lines (i.e. where fast and slow current meet). Drop-offs are also prime target locations. Ten to twenty minutes in each location is ample to tempt any resident fish.

Shore-based anglers are often limited in their ability to move locations, but can maximise results by targeting bigger snags, current edges and deeper water. Shallow, fast water does not hold many fish. Shore based anglers achieve better success at first and last light, when fish are most active. By staying longer (30-60 minutes) in each location at these peak times, feeding fish are more likely to find your bait.

BAIT COLLECTION

The ability to regularly catch quality fish from the Murrumbidgee River involves good bait. Many fisherman purchase bait, which is fine for baits such as yabbies and scrub worms, as they are relatively cheap to purchase. However, prime baits such as live shrimp and fresh bardi grubs are generally not available commercially and if they are, the price can be prohibitive. The best option is to collect your own.

SHRIMP

Freshwater shrimp appeal to all native fish species with golden perch having a particular penchant for this crustacean. Shrimp are easily captured in traps baited with soap, meat or a piece of fish. If you don't have a trap, a bucket with holes drilled through the bottom and sides (to let the water out and keep the shrimp in upon retrieval) is sufficient.

Shrimp are found throughout the Murrumbidgee River and concentrate among snags, weeds, rushes, willows and other structure in shallow water. Shrimp are more easily caught in summer than winter. In winter, shrimp can be captured more easily in warmer water bodies such as backwaters or billabongs. There are many billabongs located on or adjacent to river access sites. Provided they have water in them, shrimp are usually present.

Shrimp are agile creatures and move quickly in (and out) of traps, requiring regular checks. Handled carefully, they can be stored for short periods in non-aerated water, but will endure for long periods provided the water is aerated or changed regularly, and is kept cool. Unused shrimp freeze well for use on the next trip.

The simplest way to attach shrimp to the hook is to pierce it once straight through the tail. This keep the shrimp alive and the movement stimulates fish to bite. Several shrimp may be placed on a hook to provide a larger, more enticing bait.

YABBIES

Yabbies are a popular bait for inland anglers. Used alive and hooked through the tail they account for many Murray cod and golden perch captures. The Murrumbidgee River does hold populations of yabbies, however they are more easily collected from farm dams or irrigation channels.

Yabbies are easily captured using hoop nets baited with fresh meat or fish. Nets are checked every 10-15 minutes. Alternatively, every child's favourite way to catch yabbies is a small piece of meat tied to a metre or two of string. The string goes taut when a yabby is escaping with the bait. Retrieve the string slowly, before scooping the yabby out with your hand (for the brave) or a kitchen strainer.

Yabbies of all sizes are suitable as bait with small ones generally better for angling. The peeled tails of large yabbies are excellent bait for golden perch when threaded onto the hook. Whole yabbies are hooked through the tail (to one side avoiding the digestive tract) to ensure they remain alive Yabbies of similar size should be stored together to stop them attacking each other. Store yabbies in a container with just enough water to wet their legs (do not cover them). A leafy gum branch in the container will ensure that they stay cool and reduce mortalities.

Bardi Grubs

Larvae of the goat moth or 'bardi grub' are difficult bait to collect, but are the most effective to catch Murray cod. Most riverside reserves have gum trees growing on them. Bardi grubs live in tunnels built in the soil under these trees. Locating these tunnels requires an understanding of the moth's life cycle. During autumn storms, the grubs pupate and transform into moths where they hatch en-masse. The moths land on gum tree branches and spread eggs on the ground below. The tiny grubs burrow into the rain softened soil and build tunnels where they live for two to three years. Grubs feed on tree roots and build tunnels that can be over a metre deep and 20 mm in diameter.

When searching for grubs, a good place to start are small to medium-sized eucalypts. Inspect the base of the tree for old grub holes, or discarded shells. If grubs were there previously, the next generation are likely to still be under the ground. A layer of soil must be chipped off with a shovel to expose the hole. The grub is removed from its hole using a corkscrew on the end of a wire, a clamp-style extraction device, or for the patient - a length of long grass.

Grubs are stored in refrigerated fresh water. For long term storage, frozen grubs keep for many months. Grubs may also be stored in brine solutions, blanched in milk, or individually frozen. Grubs must be kept cold as heat quickly ruins them. Collecting bardi grubs is back-breaking work, but they are the king of baits for Murray cod.

Wood Grubs

Wood grubs are the larvae of the long horned beetle and aren't related to the bardi grub. Wood grubs bore holes into live trees, preferring willow, maple, peppercorn and kurrajong trees. They can cause infestations leading to tree death.

Wood grubs complete their life cycle in the tree. Infested trees (or parts thereof) commonly fall over or break off as the grubs bore the wood almost hollow. A chainsaw, axe or block splitter are necessary tools required to expose the grubs.

Worms

Worms are excellent bait that will often catch a fish when other options have failed. For a family outing, a bunch of garden worms will have a fish nibbling away in no time, bringing a smile to a child's face.

The worms present in compost (red wrigglers, tigers) work effectively, but they often lack the physical bulk required to tempt larger Murray cod and golden perch. Big, fat garden worms are better for this purpose, however scrub worms are ideal for river fishing. Scrub worms are long with tough skin that protects it from small pickers until a bigger fish finds the bait.

Scrub worms can be collected from the boggy edges of billabongs and springs. The specific locations they inhabit varies with the seasons, but are typically found in an area between the saturated soil (where the mud is sticky) and the crumbly dry soil. Areas with significant amounts of decaying leaf litter at the end of a drying billabong are common scrub worm habitat. In dry times, scrub worms are difficult to find and purchasing is the only option. Store scrub worms in the same soil they were taken from and ensure they are kept cool.

Bait Fishing Rigs

The classic running sinker rig works effectively in most situations. Anglers can either let the sinker run directly to the hook, or hold it away from the hook using a stopper, such as a swivel or split shot. Running sinker rigs are simple, quick and with fewer knots in the line, are less prone to failure.

Sinker weights are determined by current flow (faster current = bigger sinker). You should use just enough lead to hold your bait on the bottom.

Hook choice is determined by bait size. For example, a small bunch of worms may require a 1/0 hook, whereas a large bardi grub or yabbie, may require a 6/0 hook. Native fish have relatively large mouths, but the balance between hook and bait should be maintained. Too small a hook and the fish may reject the bait without hooking itself, and too large a hook in relation to bait size, may spook fish before they bite. Circle and 'J' hooks are effective in the Murrumbidgee River with the former being preferable as fish are generally mouth-hooked and easier to release.

CHAPTER 3
LURE FISHING

Lures fishing is an active method to catch a number of species in the Murrumbidgee River. Murray cod and golden perch readily take lures, whilst trout cod are common by-catch attacking lures with great ferocity. Other species such as silver perch, catfish, carp, trout and redfin bite lures, but they are uncommon captures.

Tackle stores display massive numbers of lures. All lures can catch fish under the right circumstances, but it's vital that lures are selected to suit the water you plan to fish. Lure types for fishing the Murrumbidgee River are of four general types. The hard-body lure, lipless crankbaits, spinnerbaits, and soft plastics. Each lure type requires specific techniques to use them correctly.

Hard Body Lures

The Riverina can be called home of the hard-body in Australia with several local companies manufacturing lures suited to fishing the Murrumbidgee River. When selecting lures at the tackle store, pay attention to the depth that each lure is rated to dive. Choose lures that dive 4 m to 6 m to when fishing the river, and lures that dive 10 m to 12 m when fishing in the deep weir pools. Lure colour is personal preference; however black/yellow and black/green are common colours.

Fishing the river with hard-body lures is simplest from a boat, but shored based anglers repeatedly casting to snags, rocks, and drop-offs will entice strikes. Boat fishers should make several casts to a structure before moving to the next snag or drop-off, or you can troll. Trolling covers more water than casting, and allows the angler to target fish that may be holding in deeper water.

When trolling, motor upstream (or downstream if the current is slow or stopped) with the lures running from 30 cm to 100 cm from the bottom. If the lure repeatedly hits the bottom, retrieve line until the lure runs in clear water. Also, if the water deepens, let line out so that the lure dives down to the 30 cm to 100 cm strike zone. Make repeated trolling runs through the deeper sections of river and concentrate efforts on the outside of river bends.

Hard body lures are also manufactured that swim along the surface. This form of fishing is done from boat or shore usually at dawn, dusk and at night when Murray cod are active. This style of fishing is exciting as Murray cod attempt to snatch the lure from the surface. More strikes are enticed by positioning surface lures adjacent to structure.

Lipless Crankbaits

Lipless crankbaits or 'bibless lures' are popular because of their versatility, the different actions that can be imparted, and a lifelike shape to tempt fussy fish. These lures are weighted to sink 'head down' requiring anglers to impart an action through the rod to maximise their effectiveness. A feature of this lure type is that most have loud rattles that appeal to Murray cod and golden perch. Fishing with lipless crankbaits differs to using bibbed lures in that they sink and are attractive to fish as they descend through the water column. This allows bibless lures to be positioned against structure and allowed to sink directly down, rather than drawing it away as required with a bibbed lure. Short, sharp ripping or jigging movements bring the rattles (and the lure) to life. Alternatively, a very slow retrieval (so the lure does not vibrate or rattle) can tempt fish on slow days.

Spinnerbaits

Spinnerbaits are a very effective casting lure. The construction of these lures allow them to be cast into complex structure (where the fish live) with a lower likelihood of snagging than a hard-body or bibless lure. The in-built buoyancy of hard-body lures requires retrieval to impart action and depth before they are of interest to fish. Conversely, spinnerbaits generally 'helicopter' as they slowly sink, which attracts bites as the lure falls through the water column. Spinnerbait retrieval should be slow as possible to keep the blades spinning. Retrieve variations can include straight winds, pauses and small jerks to add extra action to the lure. Spinnerbaits can also be trolled with heavier weighted heads suitable for this purpose.

There are numerous brands, colours and configurations of spinnerbaits. The selection in most inland tackle stores is daunting. However, choose spinnerbaits equipped with ball bearing swivels and sharp, sturdy hooks. Colour isn't vital, but black, red, purple and white are commonly used. Choose a weight that has a slow sink rate in the current flow. Too heavy and the lure plummets to the bottom. Too light and the lure will 'float' in the current. Half to three-quarter ounce is usually sufficient, depending on the blade configuration. Colorado blades are shaped like a spoon and sink slower than willow blades that resemble like a long, thin leaf.

Soft Plastic Lures

Soft plastics come in all shapes, sizes and colours. The more effective types for river use are yabby imitations and shads (the ones that look like small fish). Soft plastics are better suited for cast and retrieve fishing, similar to how spinnerbaits are used. Soft plastics can be fished slow rolled, paused, stopped, fast wind, or jigged to entice strikes. Select weights that sink slowly but are heavy enough to not 'float' in the current. Colours are not crucial but black, red and purple combinations are effective. 'Weedless' rigs are better suited to river conditions as exposed hooks in a typical jig head snag easily.

Lure Fishing Rigs

Rigging up for lure fishing requires 8-15 kg line, which can be monofilament or braid. Braided lines have the advantage of being able to distinguish bites from structure more readily, whereas the stretch in monofilament is more forgiving for novice anglers. When using braid, one to two metres of 15-20 kg monofilament or fluorocarbon leader protects the main line from abrasion. Baitcaster or overhead reels permit greater cast control than threadline or spinning reels. Reel type is not crucial, but emphasis should be placed on whether the drag system operates smoothly to avoid large fish breaking the line. Reels should be matched to a light tipped rod (with strength in the butt to slow large fish) typically rated at 3-8 kg and 170-190 cm in length.

CHAPTER 4
DE-SNAGGING

Getting snagged is common when lure fishing the Murrumbidgee River. A de-snagging tool is essential equipment to retrieve lures stuck in deep water or high in a tree. De-snaggers come in many forms, with a simple, effective version is a 20 cm length of lead-filled pipe with a continuous wire (to attach your snagged line to the lure retriever) and light chains fixed to the bottom. The de-snagger slides down the line where it knocks the lure off the snag or entangles the hooks in the chain.

Another tool used for lure retrieval, involves a long pole with a corkscrew on the end (to attach the line). This style of retriever works by sliding the pole along the snagged line until it touches the lure. The lure is then pushed off and retrieved. Pole-style lure retrievers are ideal for retrieving lures that find themselves high in a tree, and can be used to untangle hooked fish that have swum into deep cover.

Lure retrievers are essential fishing equipment and usually pay for themselves after only one trip to the river.

CHAPTER 5
REMOTE BOAT LAUNCH & RETRIEVAL

Current fishing trends favour trailer boats with casting decks, high horsepower engines, electric motor, multiple batteries and a range of accessories. These options make a boat heavy and difficult to launch and retrieve in river conditions. To launch heavy boats, river access is required via a concrete or dry, gently sloping bank and usually a 4WD. However, with some trailer modifications and using a tow or winch cable, heavy vessels can be launched and retrieved in a wide variety of conditions.

Trailer Set-up

The first step is to mount your spare wheel on the draw bar so that when the jockey wheel is removed (or swung away) the trailer is resting on this wheel. The third wheel is mounted on the draw bar with a stub axel and hub arrangement that allows the spare wheel to roll freely. Position the spare wheel so that half to one third protrudes below the draw bar to allow ground clearance for the tow hitch.

Using the jockey wheel for remote launching is not recommended. The jockey wheel's narrow diameter digs into the bank, creating stress on the tow link and jockey wheel, possibly breaking one or both of them. Jockey wheels are designed for manoeuvring trailers on concrete and bitumen, not sand or mud.

Remote Launching

Measure the distance from where the tow vehicle should stop (usually on flat ground on top of the bank) to where the boat can be floated from the trailer. The simplest way to do this is to pace out the distance from the water's edge to the top of the bank. Chock the trailer wheels and un-hitch the trailer from the vehicle so that it is resting on the spare wheel in a position where it will roll down the bank when un-chocked.

Drive your vehicle forward the same distance that was previously measured. Attach the tow link securely to the front of the trailer and also to the towbar of your vehicle. Remove the chocks and slowly reverse until the trailer is at the required launch depth. (You may need a helper to guide the trailer down to the water). Launch the boat as you would normally.

Note that a winch can be used in place of the vehicle to lower the trailer down to the water.

Remote Retrieval

With the trailer positioned at the correct depth, winch on the boat. Use caution as the trailer will rise quickly at the front when the boat reaches its pivot point on the trailer.

Once the boat is secured to the trailer, have a helper guide the trailer as you slowly drive away (or winch up). Once the boat and trailer are on flat ground, have your helper chock the wheels. You can then re-attach the trailer to the vehicle.

Use extreme caution when launching and retrieving your boat remotely. If the link between the vehicle and trailer fails, your rig will free-fall, potentially injuring the person helping manoeuvre the boat and trailer up the bank. Link system breaking strain should be many times greater than the combined boat and trailer weight.

CHAPTER 6
FISH OF THE MURRUMBIDGEE

The Murrumbidgee River between Gundagai and Balranald has excellent populations of Murray cod and golden perch. Supporting these iconic freshwater species are the protected trout cod, which are developing into a sustainable population from Narrandera upstream following a dedicated NSW DPI Fisheries recovery program. Murray cod and golden perch in the Murrumbidgee River are mostly wild fish with hatchery-reared fish contributing less than 10% of the population.

Silver perch, catfish, river blackfish, and redfin are present in smaller numbers throughout the system and are uncommon captures when compared to more popular angling species. Bony bream are ubiquitous throughout all waterways however they rarely take baits (and never lures) and are a major food source for the large predators.

European carp form a significant biomass in the Murrumbidgee River, with their numbers declining in dry years, but increasing after floods because of better spawning conditions for this species. Carp are also a major food source for large predators such as Murray cod and trout cod.

Murray cod

Murray cod (Maccullochella peelii) are Australia's largest freshwater fish reportedly growing in excess of 100 kg, though they are commonly caught around 40-65 cm (1–4 kg) with fish over 20 kg uncommon. These large, elongated, deep-bodied fish range from light to dark green on the body and back, with a very soft white underside. Smaller fish in clear water usually have the darkest colours whereas larger Murray cod or those from turbid waters have a green-grey appearance. Larger fish inhabit deep, slow moving water with plenty of structure (snags, rocks etc). Smaller fish inhabit similar water, but are also found in shallow faster moving water. There is a closed season for Murray cod from September to November inclusive. Bag and size limits apply.

Trout cod

Trout cod (Maccullachella macquariensis) grow to 80-90 cm and are commonly caught at 30-50 cm. Trout cod are elongated, deep-bodied fish that are similar in appearance to Murray cod. Features that distinguish it from Murray cod include an overhanging upper jaw, a long, broad, rounded snout, a straight head profile, and a horizontal stripe through the eye. It is generally blue-grey to dark brown on the back with a speckled pattern of dark grey to black spots. Trout cod are an aggressive fish commonly caught in rapidly flowing streams, around logs and rocky or gravel bottoms. Trout cod are a totally protected native fish species and must be returned to the water unharmed.

Golden perch

Golden perch (Macquaria ambigua) are a deep bodied fish with a distinctive concave forehead profile, protruding lower jaw and a rounded tail fin. Adults are bronze, olive or brownish overall, yellow on the ventral surface. Juveniles are silvery with scattered grey mottling on sides and dusky grey fins. Golden perch grow in excess of 10 kg, however 1 kg fish are a common capture. Bag and size limits apply.

Silver Perch

Silver perch (Bidyanus bidyanus) are rarely seen above 2 kg with most fish in the Murrumbidgee River less than 1 kg. Silver perch are recognized by a small head with the snout becoming increasingly beak-like with increasing size, equal jaws, small eyes, and a weakly forked tail. Shape varies with age – the body is elongate and slender in the young, becoming deeper and compressed in adults. Body colour in this species varies considerably. It can be black, grey, olive-greenish or gold on the back – grey to greenish or gold to silvery on the sides and white on the belly. Silver perch are omnivorous with a varied diet comprising a range of small aquatic insects, molluscs, earthworms and plant material. Silver perch are protected in the Murrumbidgee River.

Eel-Tailed or Freshwater Catfish

Freshwater catfish (Tandanus tandanus) are recognized by: a stout body; a large head flattened below with moderate-sized eyes; a ventral mouth with three pairs of barbels (whiskers) and an eel-like tail. Colouration may be grey, brown, reddish-brown, purplish or olive-green overall with whitish underparts. Catfish are found close to sand or gravel bottoms in slow moving streams, lakes and ponds with fringing vegetation. Adult catfish are carnivorous bottom feeders capable of exploiting a wide range of food sources. Caution should be taken when handling catfish as sharp spines at the dorsal and pectoral fins can inflict painful wounds. Catfish are protected in the Murrumbidgee River.

River Blackfish

River blackfish (Gadopsis marmoratus) are recognized by an elongate rounded body tapering gradually to the rounded tail, a long low dorsal fin running along two thirds of the body length, a large mouth reaching to below the eye and a lower jaw shorter than

the upper. Colour ranges from uniform dark grey overall to paler brown with irregular darker bands, blotches or mottling on sides extending to fins. The river blackfish is a carnivorous fish with a diet consisting of aquatic insects, crays and shrimp, molluscs, worms and small fishes. They grow to 45 cm, but are commonly 20-30 cm. They are a bottom dwelling fish preferring slow flowing or still areas.

European or Common Carp

Although small European carp (Cyprinus carpio) can be mistaken for goldfish (Carassius auratus), carp are distinguished by having a pair of barbels (whiskers) at each corner of their mouth. Carp have small eyes, thick lips, a forked tail and a single dorsal (top) fin with strongly serrated spines. The scales are large and thick. Some variants, known as mirrored carp, are only partly scaled, with a few very large scales in patches or along the midline. The colour of carp varies, but are usually olive green to bronze or silvery in colour with a paler underside. Carp are omnivorous, and their

diet varies depending on what is available. They consume a range of small food items such as molluscs, crustaceans, insect larvae and seeds. Carp are now the most abundant fish species in many NSW rivers, accounting for 90% of the fish biomass (i.e. the total weight of fish caught) in some areas. Any carp captured should not be returned to the water. No bag or size limits apply.

Redfin or English Perch

Redfin (Perca fluviatilis) are a relatively elongated fish with a slightly forked tail, large mouth, six or more broad black vertical bands across the back tapering at the sides, two separate dorsal fins (the first with a distinct rear black blotch) and a reddish tinge

to lower fins and margin of the tail. Adults are olive green to grey on back, greenish to silvery on sides with white belly. Redfin are an introduced species to Australian waters and may have contributed to the decline of some native species. As such, they must not be returned to the water if caught. Redfin are commonly caught at 0.5 kg, but grow in excess of 2 kg. They are recognised for their good eating qualities. No bag or size limits apply.

Bony bream

Bony bream or hairback herring (Nematalosa erebi) are a small silvery fish characterised by a blunt snout, forked tail, serrated edge on the belly scales and a long filament at the posterior end of the dorsal fin. They occur in a variety of habitats, but most common in the shallows of still or slow-flowing streams and rivers. Bony bream eat algae and detritus; however planktonic items, mainly crustaceans, also form part of their diet. Large adults up to 1 kg are occasionally caught by anglers. No bag or size limits apply.

Brown Trout

Imported from England in the 1860's, the brown trout (Salmo trutta) has variable colouration depending on habitat and age. It is generally silver through brown to olive overall but darker along the back. Dark spots are present along the back and sides but these can sometimes be indistinct. Most spots are surrounded by a pale halo and are often red below the mid line. Bag and size limits apply.

Rainbow Trout

Rainbow trout (Oncorhynchus mykiss) were introduced to Australia several years after the brown trout. Colour varies from silver to pale olive-brown overall (in riverine fish) and is darker along the back. The fish has spots on head, body, top fin and tail fin which can sometimes be inconspicuous. Typically the fish has a red or orange patch on the gill cover which extends as a stripe

along the mid-line. Rainbow trout are regularly caught in the Murrumbidgee upstream from Wagga Wagga in fast flowing sections of the river. Bag and size limits apply.

Murray Crayfish

Murray crayfish (Euastacus armatus) are one of over twenty species of spiny crayfish found in NSW. They occur in the Murray and Murrumbidgee rivers and many of their tributaries. Commonly known as freshwater crays or lobsters, they are recognised and distinguished from yabbies by their larger size (up to 2 kg), distinctive white claws and body spines. There are complex NSW DPI Fisheries regulations regarding Murray crayfish. Check with your local NSW DPI Fisheries office for current regulations.

Crayfishing

Murray crayfish can be taken during the months of June, July and August in the following waters only: Murrumbidgee River and its tributaries (excluding Old Man Creek) from the Hume Highway road bridge at Gundagai downstream to a line 100 m upstream of the weir face of Berembed Weir. Additionally, the taking of berried females and the removal of heads, tails or claws of Murray Crayfish in, on or adjacent to waters, is prohibited. The minimum size is 10 cm occipital-carapace length (OCL) with a maximum length of 12 cm OCL. The bag limit is 2 per day and 4 in possession.

These (and other specific) regulations are necessary to protect the species which can take up to eight years to mature. Murray crayfish are generally found in relatively deep water adjacent to structure such as mud banks, clay drop-offs and snags. To catch crayfish, hoop nets are baited with meat, fish or offal and lowered to the river bed, where crayfish accumulate for an easy meal. To check a hoop net, approach from downstream and when the rope is vertical, retrieve rapidly, enabling water pressure to hold crayfish in the bottom of the net.

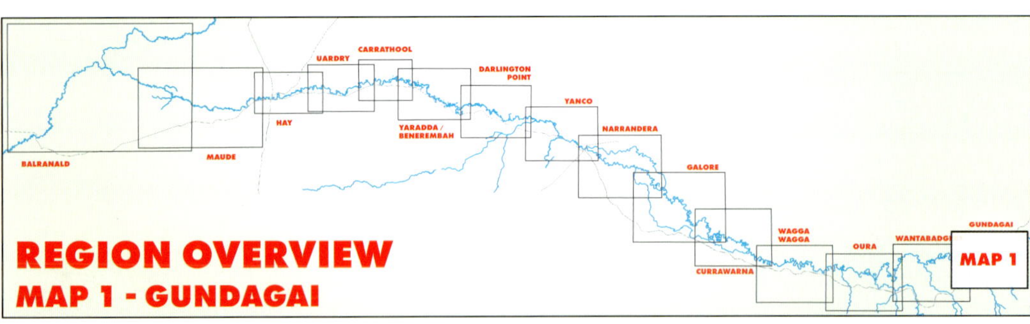

REGION OVERVIEW
MAP 1 - GUNDAGAI
BALRANALD
MAUDE
HAY
UARDRY
CARRATHOOL
YARADDA / BENEREMBAH
DARLINGTON POINT
YANCO
NARRANDERA
GALORE
WAGGA WAGGA
CURRAWARNA
OURA
GUNDAGAI
MAP 1

Nangus
Oura Road
Oaks Hill Road
Soldier Settlers Road
Soldier Settlers Road
Nangus Tip Road
Nangus Road
Backstation Creek
LIME KILN TSR
6
Murrumbidgee River
Southcorp Winery
Old Hume Highway Road
Adelong Creek
Adelong Creek Road
HUME HIGHWAY
HUME HIGHWAY
Tumblong Road
N
NE
E
SE
S
SW
W
NW
Kilometres
0
1
2
3
4
5

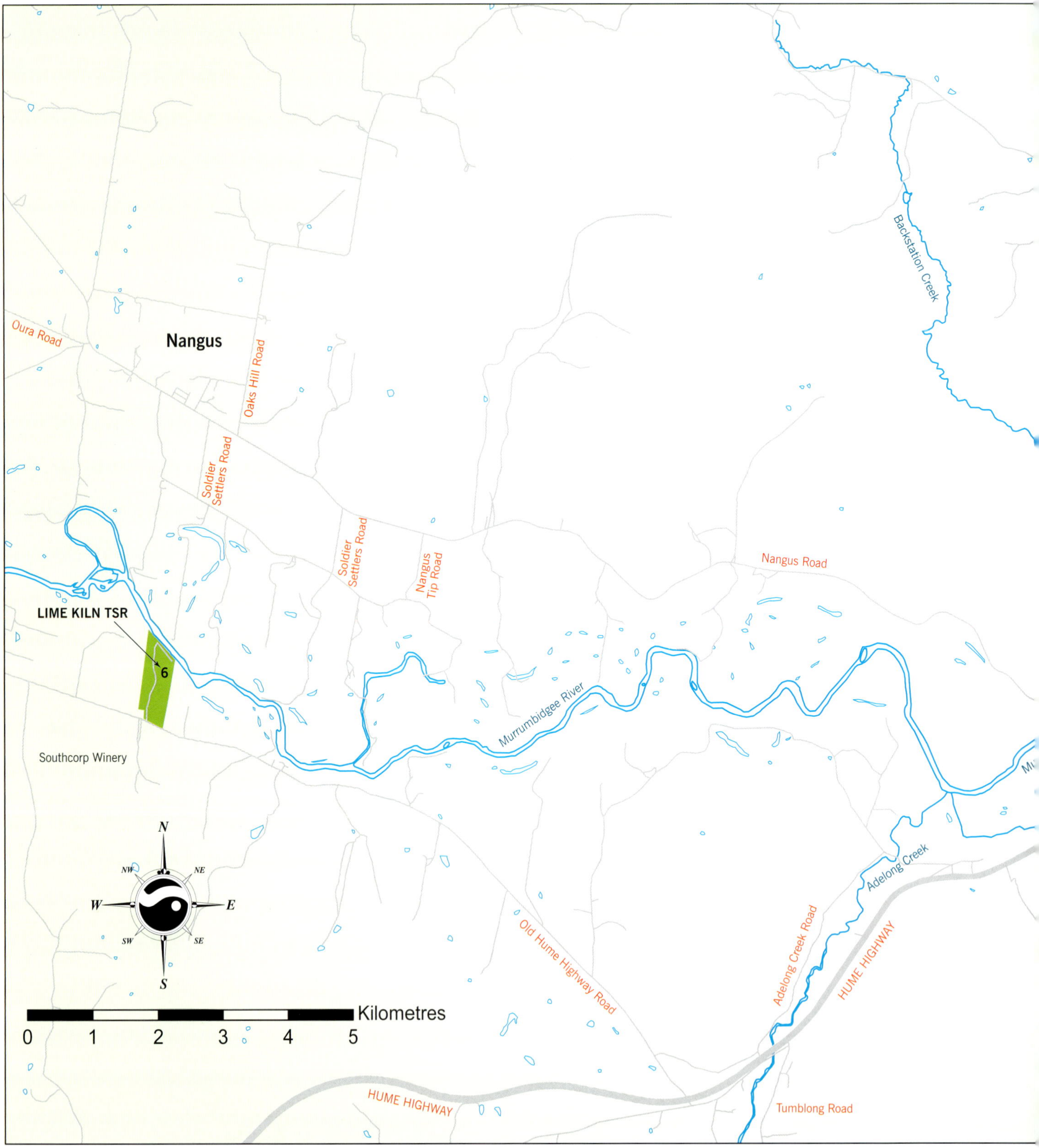

CHAPTER 7
GUNDAGAI REGION

Gundagai is located at the foothills of the Snowy Mountains and is the gateway to the Riverina. Gundagai is well known in bush verse, which stems from the fact that Five Mile Creek, to the north of town, was a popular meeting place with drovers, shearers and bush travellers. Riverboats used to travel as far as Gundagai, however it proved to be too far upstream to make the venture commercially viable. The rolling hills surrounding Gundagai make this a very picturesque part of the Murrumbidgee with the river banks lined with willows, red gums and she-oaks. The river is typically fast and featured by stone riffles and sand bars with slower, deep pools in between.

1. NORTH GUNDAGAI COMMON

ACCESS ROADS	★★★★★
BOAT RAMP	NONE
CAMPING	★★★
SWIMMING	★★★★
SHORE BASED FISHING	★
TOILETS	NONE
SHADE	★★★★
BINS	NONE
BARBEQUES	NONE
TABLES/SEATS	NONE

DIRECTIONS

The entrance is located on O.I. Bell Road, North Gundagai (opposite Landon St).

GPS 35.070143 148.106637

North Gundagai Common features broad grassland expanses and large river red gums. The river is fenced off, however gates at various locations provide pedestrian access to the water. There are no facilities such as tables, toilets and barbeques apart from those provided at the showground arena. Swimming is good in places, particularly adjacent to the rail bridge where shallow, slow-flowing water creates ideal conditions. Shore based fishing is limited because of mostly shallow water.

2. SOUTH GUNDAGAI RECREATION RESERVE

DIRECTIONS

From Mount Street, turn west into Ridge Street. Turn right at the T intersection and proceed into the reserve.

GPS -35.074872 148.102502

ACCESS ROADS	★★★★★
BOAT RAMP	★★★★
CAMPING	★★
SWIMMING	★★★★
SHORE BASED FISHING	★★
TOILETS	NONE
SHADE	★★★★
BINS	NONE
BARBEQUES	NONE
TABLES/SEATS	NONE

Located in the heart of Gundagai, the South Gundagai Recreation Reserve offers excellent boat launching facilities from the boat ramp or across the stony beach. The stone and gravel base provides all weather access for boat launching. Access is excellent with well-formed tracks allowing 2WD all weather driveability. There are many open, flat campsites. The best shore based angling is located away from the beach area. The beach offers excellent swimming and is a popular venue during summer.

3. NORTH GUNDAGAI BOAT RAMP

DIRECTIONS

Take the Nangus Road east of North Gundagai & pass over the Jones Creek Bridge. The entrance is 700 m west of this bridge.

GPS -35.070433 148.091590

ACCESS ROADS	★★★★
BOAT RAMP	★★★★
CAMPING	★★★
SWIMMING	★
SHORE BASED FISHING	★★★
TOILETS	NONE
SHADE	★★★★★
BINS	NONE
BARBEQUES	NONE
TABLES/SEATS	NONE

North Gundagai Boat Ramp has a concrete boat ramp for launching trailer boats. Launching of large boats during low water levels requires 4WD. The access road is suitable for 2WD vehicles in all weather conditions. Camping is good with large, flat sites and ample shade. Shore based fishing is restricted with poor access to many locations. Fast current and shallow stone riffles are hazardous to navigation.

4. NORTH GUNDAGAI

DIRECTIONS

Take the Nangus Road east of North Gundagai and pass over the Jones Creek Bridge. The entrance is located 1.7 km west of this bridge.

GPS -35.075562 148.085594

ACCESS ROADS	★★
BOAT RAMP	★★★
CAMPING	★★
SWIMMING	★★★
SHORE BASED FISHING	★★★
TOILETS	NONE
SHADE	★★★★
BINS	NONE
BARBEQUES	NONE
TABLES/SEATS	NONE

North Gundagai is featured by braided, sandy tracks and limited sites for camping. The access road is 4WD with a difficult trailer boat launch from the stony beach or the dirt ramp located toward the middle of the reserve. The shoreline offers good angling opportunities.

5. RANKINS TSR

DIRECTIONS

Take the Nangus Road east of North Gundagai and pass over the Jones Creek Bridge. The entrances are located at 2.7 km and 3.1 km west of this bridge.

GPS -35.081973 148.078571

ACCESS ROADS	★★★
BOAT RAMP	★★
CAMPING	★★★
SWIMMING	★★★
SHORE BASED FISHING	★
TOILETS	NONE
SHADE	★★★
BINS	NONE
BARBEQUES	NONE
TABLES/SEATS	NONE

The access roads are 2WD in dry weather. Boat launching is available from the stony beach. Camping is limited with few available locations (there is an excellent site upstream of the beach and another downstream of the beach). Trees along the foreshore provide excellent shade. Swimming is available being both scenic and secluded. Shore based fishing is difficult with better fish habitat downstream of the beach.

6. LIME KILN TSR

DIRECTIONS

The entrance is located 7.6km from Tenandra Road (i.e. the low level bridge) toward the Hume Highway. From the Hume Hwy proceed 10.7km along the Old Hume Highway Road to the entrance.

GPS -35.097890 147.901522

ACCESS ROADS	★★★★
BOAT RAMP	NONE
CAMPING	★★★★★
SWIMMING	★
SHORE BASED FISHING	★★★★★
TOILETS	NONE
SHADE	★★★★★
BINS	NONE
BARBEQUES	NONE
TABLES/SEATS	NONE

Lime Kiln TSR offers excellent camping with silky oak lining the shoreline and scattered red gums providing shade. The access road is smooth and suitable for 2WD when dry. The bank is steep for the length of the reserve with no trailer boat launch site. Shore based fishing is excellent. Lime Kiln isn't a suitable swimming area because of steep banks and fast-flowing water. Flat, open campsites are suitable for large groups and caravans.

REGION OVERVIEW
MAP 2 - WANTABADGERY
BALRANALD
MAUDE
HAY
UARDRY
CARRATHOOL
YARADDA / BENEREMBAH
DARLINGTON POINT
YANCO
NARRANDERA
GALORE
WAGGA WAGGA
CURRAWARNA
OURA
MAP 2
WANTABADGERY
GUNDAGAI

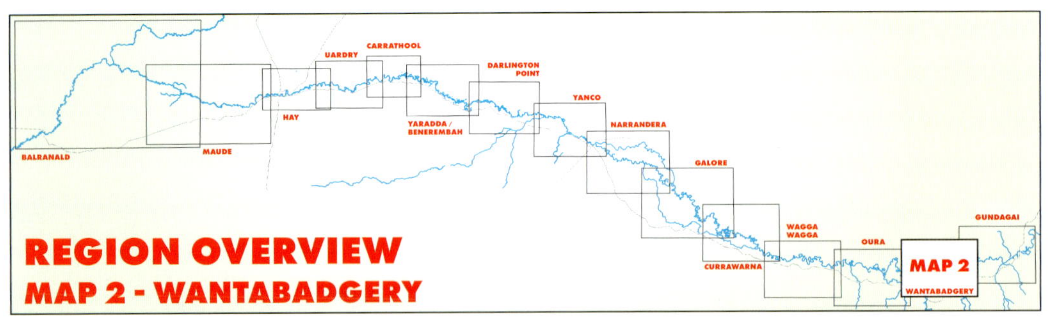

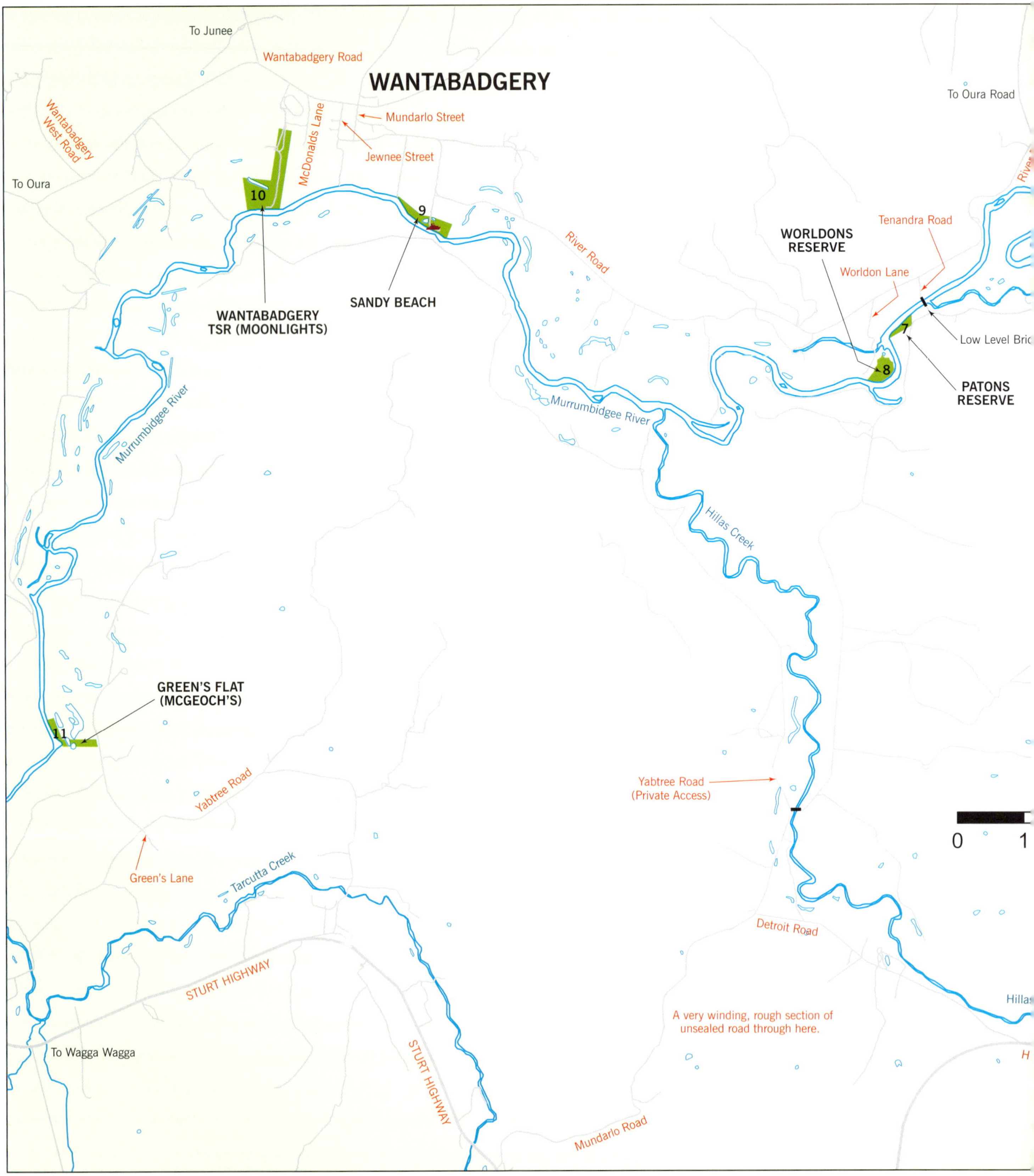

WANTABADGERY
To Junee
Wantabadgery Road
Wantabadgery West Road
McDonalds Lane
Mundarlo Street
Jewnee Street
To Oura
To Oura Road
10
WANTABADGERY TSR (MOONLIGHTS)
9
SANDY BEACH
River Road
Tenandra Road
WORLDONS RESERVE
Worldon Lane
Low Level Bri
7
8
PATONS RESERVE
Murrumbidgee River
Murrumbidgee River
Hillas Creek
GREEN'S FLAT (MCGEOCH'S)
11
Yabtree Road
Green's Lane
Yabtree Road (Private Access)
0
1
Tarcutta Creek
Detroit Road
STURT HIGHWAY
STURT HIGHWAY
To Wagga Wagga
A very winding, rough section of unsealed road through here.
Mundarlo Road
Hillas

WANTABADGERY REGION

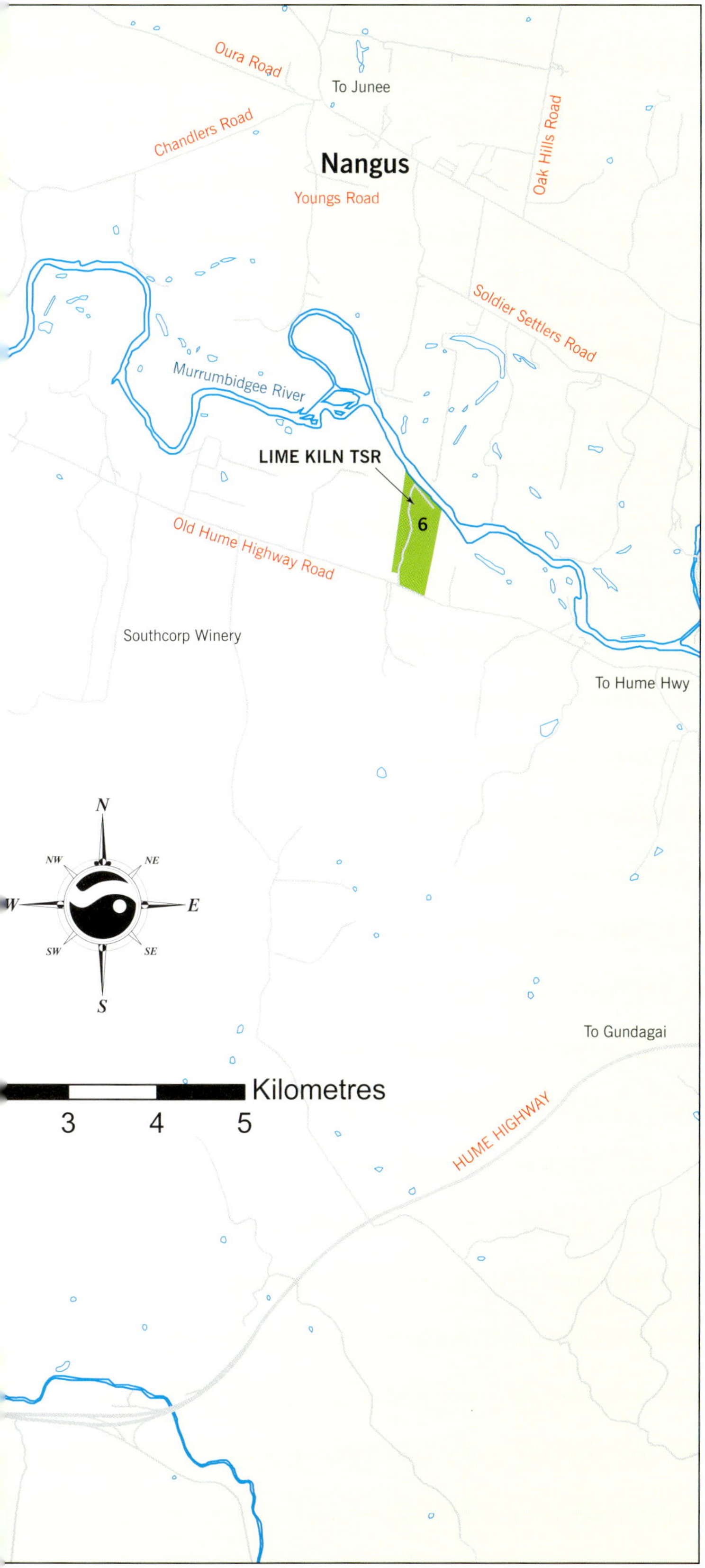

Wantabadgery is a region made famous by the notorious bushranger Captain Moonlight who held up Wantabadgery Station after he and his men were refused work. For this reason Wantabadgery TSR is known locally as 'Moonlights'. This region is a rich agricultural area with rolling hills and river plains playing host to sheep, cattle, cereal crops, and canola. The northern and southern banks are linked by a low-level bridge at Mundarlo allowing access to reserves on both sides of the river and means to travel between Wantabadgery/Nangus and the Sturt Highway.

Oura Road
To Junee
Chandlers Road
Oak Hills Road
Nangus
Youngs Road
Soldier Settlers Road
Murrumbidgee River
LIME KILN TSR
6
Old Hume Highway Road
Southcorp Winery
To Hume Hwy
N
NW
NE
W
E
SW
SE
S
To Gundagai
Kilometres
3 4 5
HUME HIGHWAY

7. PATONS RESERVE

DIRECTIONS

The entrance gate is hidden below the road 300 m west of Tenandra Road (i.e. the low level bridge). The reserve is accessed through large granite boulders.

GPS -35.083275 147.819786

ACCESS ROADS	★★★
BOAT RAMP	★
CAMPING	★★★★
SWIMMING	★
SHORE BASED FISHING	★★★★
TOILETS	NONE
SHADE	★
BINS	NONE
BARBEQUES	NONE
TABLES/SEATS	NONE

Shore based fishing is excellent with submerged snags creating ideal fish habitat. Trailer boat launching is not available as no defined ramp exists. The reserve offers good camping and easy access to the waterfront, however shade is limited away from the water, as the reserve is largely devoid of trees.

8. WORLDONS RESERVE

DIRECTIONS

Turn south into Worldon Lane (750 m west of Tenandra Road) from River Road. Follow the track past the front of the house and continue into the reserve.

GPS -35.080282 147.813463

Worldons Reserve is a large area that is predominately sand and gravel. Access roads are 4WD. Boat launching is a difficult 4WD launch across a mud/stone beach at the upstream boundary. The boat launch area (at the upstream boundary) is a shallow backwater off the main river. Low water levels can make boat launching impossible. The best camping and swimming location is near the downstream boundary where the sandy beach provides good access to the water and a flat area for camping.

ACCESS ROADS	★★★
BOAT RAMP	★
CAMPING	★★
SWIMMING	★★★
SHORE BASED FISHING	★★★
TOILETS	NONE
SHADE	★★★★
BINS	NONE
BARBEQUES	NONE
TABLES/SEATS	NONE

9. SANDY BEACH

DIRECTIONS

Sandy Beach is 7.8 km west of Worldon Lane and 2.9km east of Wantabadgery.

GPS -35.067418 147.740209

ACCESS ROADS	★★★★★
BOAT RAMP	★★★★★
CAMPING	★★★★★
SWIMMING	★★★
SHORE BASED FISHING	★★★★
TOILETS	★★★★★
SHADE	★★★★★
BINS	★★★★★
BARBEQUES	NONE
TABLES/SEATS	★★★★★

Sandy Beach is a well-manicured reserve offering a concrete boat ramp, toilets, tables with shades, rubbish bins and open areas suitable for large camps. Shored based fishing is good with accessible fish holding structure along the foreshore. Boat navigation is good but care should be taken to avoid sand/stone bars and mid-river snags, particularly when water levels are low. The access road is well maintained and suitable for caravans. Sandy Beach is an ideal family campsite or short-stay location for caravans.

10. WANTABADGERY TSR (MOONLIGHTS)

ACCESS ROADS	★★★
BOAT RAMP	★★★
CAMPING	★★
SWIMMING	★★
SHORE BASED FISHING	★★
TOILETS	NONE
SHADE	★
BINS	NONE
BARBEQUES	NONE
TABLES/SEATS	NONE

DIRECTIONS

Turn into McDonalds Lane 500 m west of Wantabadgery. Turn left once through the double gates (900 m from entrance), past the cemetery on right, to the single gate 300 m further on. Proceed through this gate for 1 km to the river.

GPS -35.056753 147.715943

Wantabadgery TSR (commonly known as Moonlights) is a barren reserve with few trees. The access road is 2WD in dry weather, but requires 4WD in wet weather. Boat launching is via a gently sloping gully using 4WD or remote launch. Shore based fishing is moderate with fish habitat present along the waterfront. The reserve is an ideal location to pick up canoeists paddling downstream from Sandy Beach.

REGION OVERVIEW
MAP 3 - OURA
BALRANALD
MAUDE
HAY
UARDRY
CARRATHOOL
YARADDA / BENEREMBAH
DARLINGTON POINT
YANCO
NARRANDERA
GALORE
WAGGA WAGGA
CURRAWARNA
OURA
WANTABADGERY
GUNDAGAI
MAP 3

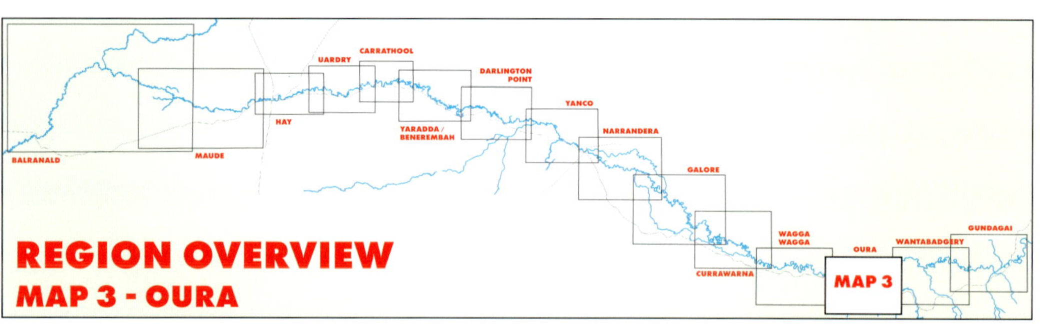

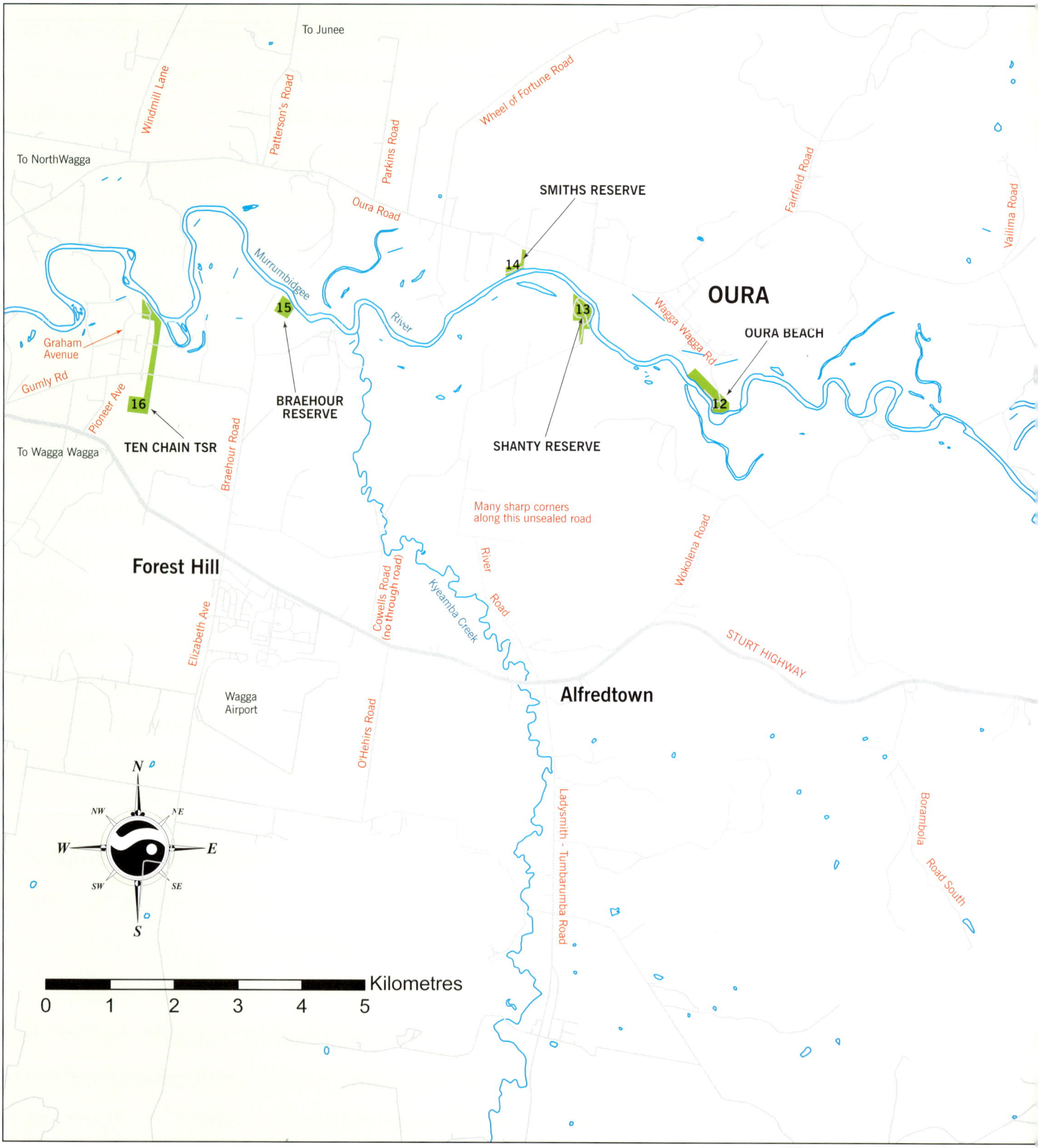

To Junee
Windmill Lane
Patterson's Road
Parkins Road
Wheel of Fortune Road
To NorthWagga
Oura Road
SMITHS RESERVE
Fairfield Road
Vailima Road
Murrumbidgee
River
OURA
14
15
13
12
16
Graham Avenue
Gumly Rd
Pioneer Ave
Wagga Wagga Rd
OURA BEACH
BRAEHOUR RESERVE
TEN CHAIN TSR
To Wagga Wagga
Braehour Road
SHANTY RESERVE
Many sharp corners along this unsealed road
Forest Hill
River Road
Wokolena Road
Cowells Road (no through road)
Kyeamba Creek
Elizabeth Ave
STURT HIGHWAY
Alfredtown
Wagga Airport
O'Hehirs Road
Ladysmith - Tumbarumba Road
Borambola Road South
N
NW
NE
W
E
SW
SE
S
0
1
2
3
4
5
Kilometres

OURA REGION

Oura marks the transition in topography from the hills of Gundagai and Wantabadgery upstream, to the river floodplain as you near Wagga Wagga. Located just upstream of Wagga Wagga, this region offers several access points to the river on both northern and southern banks and also encompasses Wagga's airport. The small hamlet of Oura is located in the midst of this region and offers excellent camping and a large sandy beach which is popular for picnickers and for travellers to camp overnight. The river becomes deeper as you move downstream and is featured by sandy beaches, tree lined banks and stony riffle beds.

To Wantabadgery
Skeltons Road
Murrumbidgee River
11
GREENS FLAT (MCGEOCH'S)
Yabtree Road
Green's Lane
Borambola Road North
McGeochs Road North
Tarcutta Creek
Borambola Sport and Recreation Centre
Windamarra Rd
Martins Rd
Coreinbob Creek
Mates Gully Road
Mates Gully Creek

11. GREEN'S FLAT (MCGEOCH'S)

ACCESS ROADS	★★★
BOAT RAMP	★★
CAMPING	★★★★
SWIMMING	★★★
SHORE BASED FISHING	★★★
TOILETS	NONE
SHADE	★★★
BINS	NONE
BARBEQUES	NONE
TABLES/SEATS	NONE

DIRECTIONS

Turn from the Sturt Hwy into Windamarra Road – turn right after 600m, across the Tarcutta Creek at bridge (1.7 km) and continue over hill (4.6 km) before turning left at Massadon farm sign. The entrance is a further 1.6km on the left through a pair of white double gates. Proceed along the dirt track and through the second gate into the reserve.

GPS -35.138740 147.684387

Access to Green's Flat (commonly known as McGeoch's) is 2WD in dry weather across reasonable dirt tracks. 4WD is required in wet conditions. Boat launching is 4WD or remote launch. Large trailer boats are difficult to launch at this site. Camping is good with open spaces and large trees providing shade. Green's Flat is a secluded reserve with excellent boat fishing. Shore based fishing is good along the waterfront, but is best at the reserve boundaries.

12. OURA BEACH

DIRECTIONS

Turn into Oura village. Continue along Wagga Wagga Rd for 1.3 km until the end. Turn right at Oura Beach signpost.

GPS -35.118417 147.543553

ACCESS ROADS	★★★★★
BOAT RAMP	★★★
CAMPING	★★★★★
SWIMMING	★★★★★
SHORE BASED FISHING	★★★
TOILETS	★★★★★
SHADE	★★★★★
BINS	★★★★★
BARBEQUES	NONE
TABLES/SEATS	★★★★★

Oura Beach is a scenic, well-maintained area suited to family picnics and camping. It offers easy access on groomed roads, toilet facilities, metal tables, fireplaces, good shade and an excellent beach for swimming. The beach offers trailer boat launching, however 4WD is recommended. Shore based fishing is good with better habitat upstream and downstream of the beach. Navigation is restricted during low water by sand/stone bars.

13. SHANTY RESERVE

DIRECTIONS

Turn from the Sturt Highway at Alfredtown (i.e. the service station) into River Road. Proceed 6.0 km along the dirt road to the entrance.

GPS -35.120520 147.510561

ACCESS ROADS	★★★
BOAT RAMP	★★★
CAMPING	★★★
SWIMMING	★★★★★
SHORE BASED FISHING	★★★
TOILETS	NONE
SHADE	★★★★★
BINS	NONE
BARBEQUES	NONE
TABLES/SEATS	NONE

The Shanty is a large reserve with numerous internal tracks created by 4WD's and motorbike riders. The reserve features a large, stony beach that provides good boat launching and excellent swimming. Camping space is limited, however several good sites are available. The long riverfront provides access to many angling locations with deeper sections above and below the stony beach being ideal.

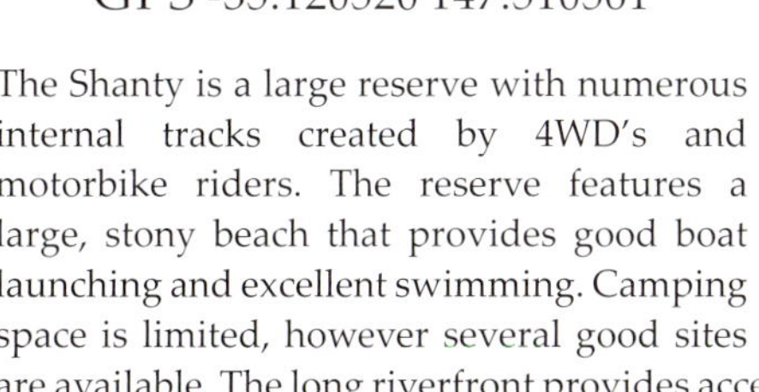

14. SMITHS RESERVE

ACCESS ROADS	★★★
BOAT RAMP	★★
CAMPING	★★★★
SWIMMING	★★
SHORE BASED FISHING	★★★★
TOILETS	NONE
SHADE	★★★
BINS	NONE
BARBEQUES	NONE
TABLES/SEATS	NONE

DIRECTIONS

Entrance gate is 2.3 km west of Oura and 2.2 km east of Patterson's Road along the Oura Road.

GPS -35.103976 147.510413

The track through Smith's Reserve is 2WD, but 4WD when wet. Boat launching is available at the upstream end of the stony beach. Caution should be taken in wet weather as the steep slope to the shore becomes slippery. Shore based angling is excellent with a clay drop-off along much of the waterfront. Shady campsites are limited to the waterfront or at the eastern boundary. The river

15. BRAEHOUR RESERVE

ACCESS ROADS	★★★
BOAT RAMP	★★
CAMPING	★★
SWIMMING	★★★
SHORE BASED FISHING	★★★
TOILETS	NONE
SHADE	★★★★
BINS	NONE
BARBEQUES	NONE
TABLES/SEATS	NONE

DIRECTIONS

Turn north from the Sturt Highway at Forest Hill into Braehour Road. Proceed 4.2 km to the entrance.

GPS -35.110129 147.466952

Braehour Reserve can be accessed by 2WD, but tracks are 4WD when wet. The reserve offers several shored based angling sites with deep water and submerged snags. Camping is better at the upstream end of the reserve. Boat launching is available for trailer boats using 4WD or remote launch. The reserve is an ideal drop-off point for canoeists paddling downstream to Wagga Wagga.

16. TEN CHAIN TSR

ACCESS ROADS	★★
BOAT RAMP	★★★
CAMPING	★★
SWIMMING	★★★
SHORE BASED FISHING	★★★
TOILETS	NONE
SHADE	★★★★
BINS	NONE
BARBEQUES	NONE
TABLES/SEATS	NONE

DIRECTIONS

Turn from the Sturt Highway into Pioneer Avenue. Proceed for 1 km and turn right at the T intersection into Gumly Road. Follow Gumly Road (past Graham Avenue) as it continues around a left hand bend (i.e. the entrance to Ten Chain TSR) and proceed north to the river.

GPS -35.113746 147.446149

Ten Chain TSR has limited camping areas, with 4WD recommended as the tracks are rough. Large boats can be 4WD launched directly off the trailer. In low water (when the beach is exposed), 4WD can drive across the beach to launch. Ten Chain offers good swimming with shallow water and relatively slow current. Angling opportunities are better away from the boat ramp area.

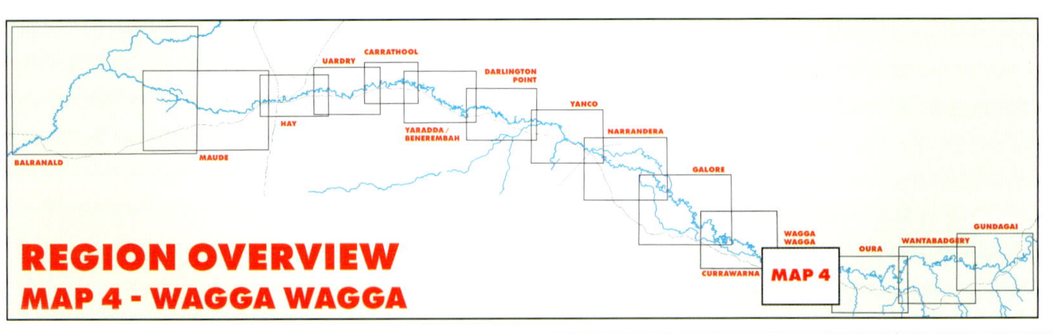

REGION OVERVIEW
MAP 4 - WAGGA WAGGA
BALRANALD
MAUDE
HAY
UARDRY
CARRATHOOL
YARADDA / BENEREMBAH
DARLINGTON POINT
YANCO
NARRANDERA
GALORE
WAGGA WAGGA
CURRAWARNA
MAP 4
OURA
WANTABADGERY
GUNDAGAI

Tooyal Road
Macks Road
Cobdens Road
Electricity Substation
Euberta
O'Sheas Road
Mack's Lane
Fletchers Lane
Eldershaws Road
Old Narrandera Road
River Road
Siselys Road
MILLERS LANE RESERVE
KOHLHAGEN'S BEACH
RIVER ROAD RESERVE
GOBBA TSR
27
River Road
30
29
Millers Lane
Poachers Lane
Toms Street
24
Gobb
Bric
Kohlhagens Road
YARRAGUNDRY TSR (ARMSTRONG'S)
28
Armstrongs Rd
ASHMONT RESERVE
26
To Collingullie
11 Mile Rd
Gormans Road
STURT HIGHWAY
25
FROG HOLLOW
Roach Road
McNickle Rd
Edward St West
Cummins Rd
Cloughs Road
Yarragundry Road
Churches Plain Road
Kapooka Road
Olympic Way
WAGGA WAGG
N
NE
E
SE
S
SW
W
NW
0
1
2
3
4
5
Kilometres

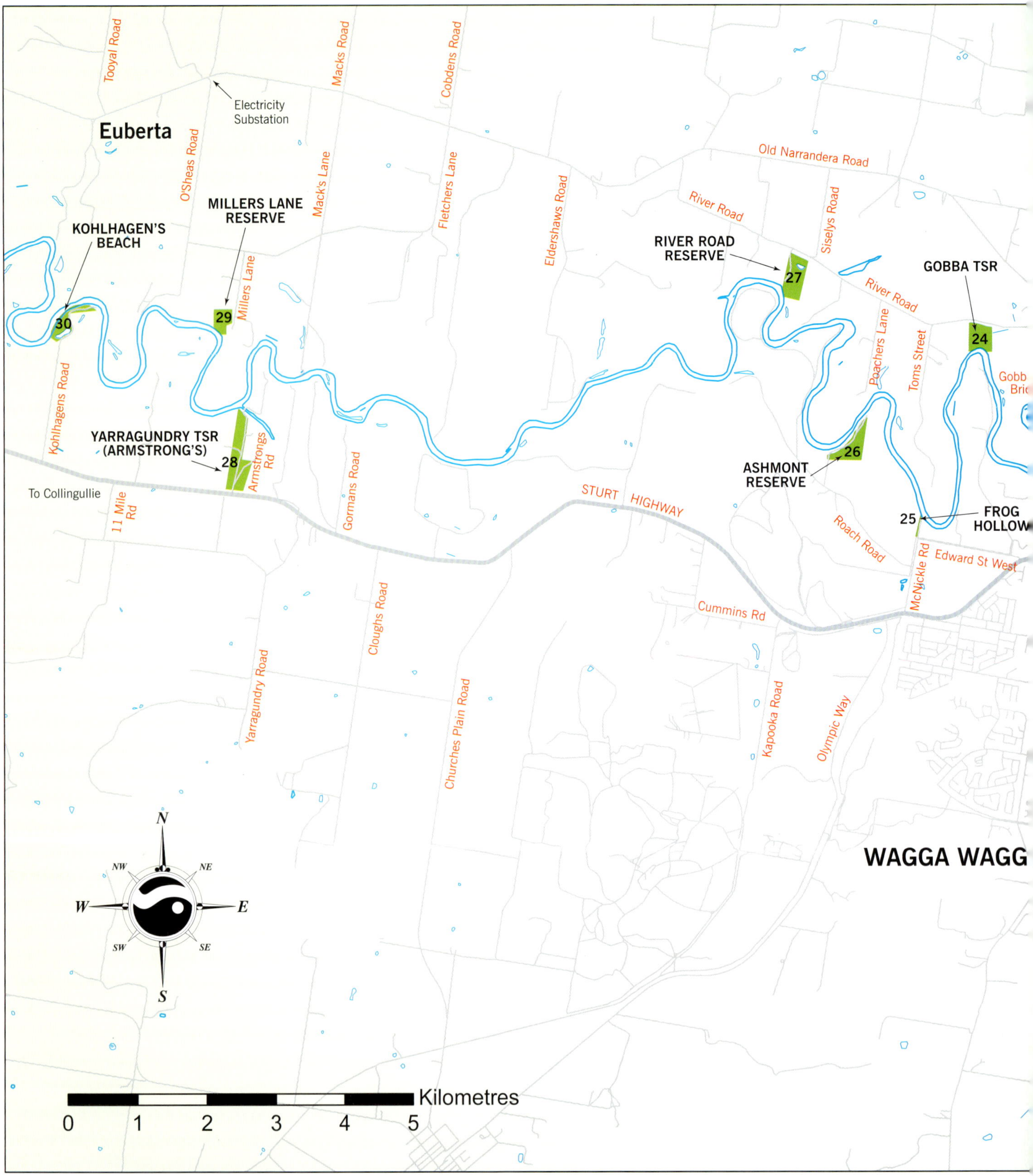

WAGGA WAGGA REGION

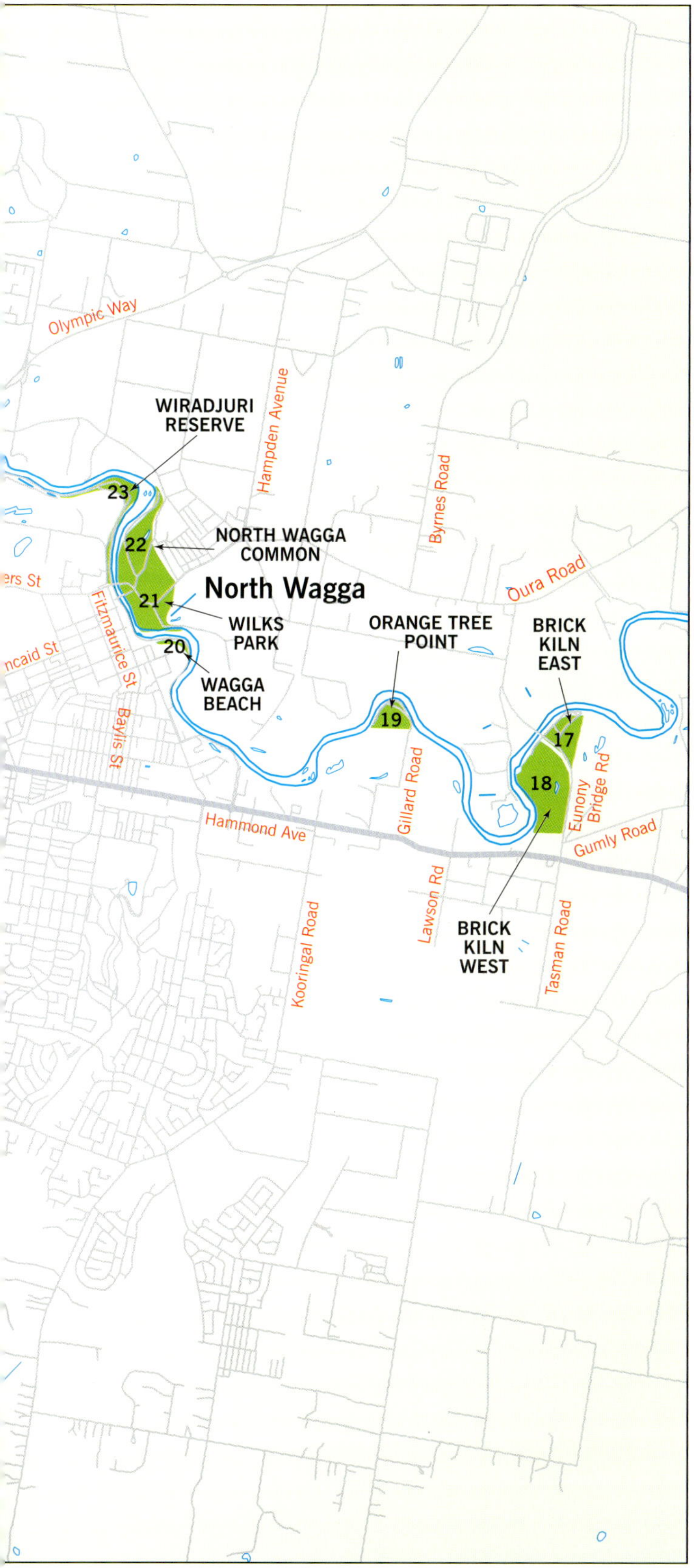

Wagga Wagga is NSW largest inland city with a population of 65,000 people. The city was founded as an intersection of the north-south track between NSW and Victoria and the east-west track along the Murrumbidgee. Paddle steamers operated to Wagga Wagga up until 1905, highlighting the integral part the river played in Wagga's history. Ten reserves are located within the cities boundaries, most of which are large enough to accommodate the outdoor needs of a large city. In particular, Wagga Beach and Wiradjuri Reserve are popular summer locations for families. The river through Wagga is navigable for most of the year, with downstream becoming deeper and slower.

17. BRICK KILN EAST

ACCESS ROADS	★★★
BOAT RAMP	★★
CAMPING	★★★
SWIMMING	★★★★
SHORE BASED FISHING	★★★
TOILETS	NONE
SHADE	★★★★
BINS	NONE
BARBEQUES	NONE
TABLES / SEATS	NONE

DIRECTIONS

Turn from the Sturt Highway into Eunony Bridge Rd (Carriage House Motel on corner) and proceed 1.3 km to the reserve on the right (100 m before bridge).

GPS -35.114868 147.420397

Brick Kiln East is characterised by a riverside track that provides excellent access to numerous shore based fishing and swimming locations. Boat launching is available using 4WD or remote launch at the sloping bank near the middle of the reserve. 4WD activity has created deep holes and ruts throughout the reserve and care should be taken when driving. The roads are 2WD when dry, but slippery when wet. Camping is good with flat, open sites under shady trees.

18. BRICK KILN WEST

DIRECTIONS

Turn from the Sturt Highway into Eunony Bridge Road (Carriage House Motel on corner) and proceed 0.4 km to the entrance on the left.

GPS -35.121519 147.421706

Brick Kiln West has a network of tracks that provide river access in a range of locations. These locations vary from high, steep banks, to beach areas. The tracks are generally rough with 4WD activity creating deep holes and ruts, however the river is accessible by 2WD when dry (4WD when wet). Camping is good with open, flat areas under shady trees, particularly at the beach area located toward the middle of the reserve. The beach area allows trailer boat launching using 4WD or remote launch, and offers the best swimming with slow, shallow water. Shore based fishing is good with access to a range of suitable habitats.

ACCESS ROADS	★★
BOAT RAMP	★★★
CAMPING	★★★
SWIMMING	★★★★
SHORE BASED FISHING	★★★
TOILETS	NONE
SHADE	★★★★
BINS	NONE
BARBEQUES	NONE
TABLES / SEATS	NONE

19. ORANGE TREE POINT

ACCESS ROADS	★★
BOAT RAMP	★★★
CAMPING	★★★★
SWIMMING	★★★
SHORE BASED FISHING	★★★
TOILETS	★★
SHADE	★★★★★
BINS	NONE
BARBEQUES	NONE
TABLES/SEATS	NONE

DIRECTIONS

Turn from the Sturt Highway into Gillard Road (550 m east of the Kooringal Road roundabout). Proceed 1.1 km down the dirt road past Tarcoola Turf Farm into the reserve.

GPS -35.117757 147.402158

The location of Orange Tree Point on Wagga's outskirts makes it a popular reserve. The main track is 2WD when dry, but is rough near the entrance, improving as you near the river. Boat launching is via a reasonable dirt ramp toward the western end of the reserve along the main track. This ramp is suitable for 4WD launching in low water. The reserve has ample open space and large shady trees for many campsites. A pit toilet provides the only amenities.

20. WAGGA BEACH

DIRECTIONS

The entrance is located at the eastern end of Johnson Street, Wagga Wagga.

GPS -35.108091 147.374337

ACCESS ROADS	★★★★★
BOAT RAMP	NONE
CAMPING	NONE
SWIMMING	★★★★★
SHORE BASED FISHING	★★★
TOILETS	★★★★★
SHADE	★★★★★
BINS	★★★★★
BARBEQUES	★★★★★
TABLES/SEATS	★★★★★

Wagga Beach is a popular swimming location in summer. It has sealed road access and a large area for parking boats, trailers or caravans. The grounds are well-maintained by Wagga Wagga City Council offering electric barbeques, a serviced toilet block, tables and chairs, and excellent shade. The Wiradjuri Walking Track (which passes through the beach) runs parallel to the river for approximately 12 km offering many excellent locations for shore-based fishing. A popular location for swimming is 'The Rocks' located 500 m upstream, which is also a good angling location with a natural rock bar creating swirling eddies in the current. No boat launching is available at Wagga Beach.

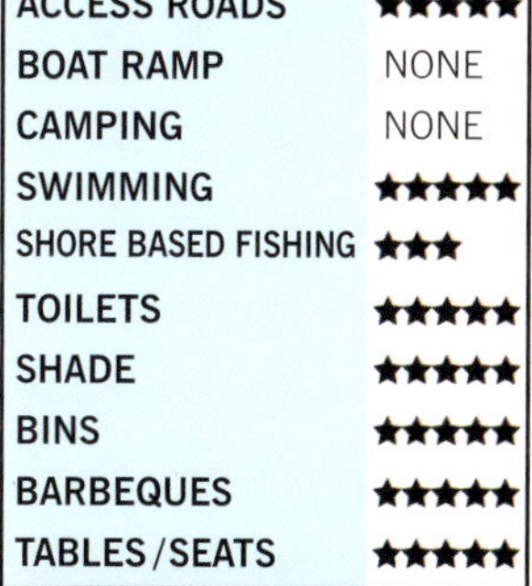

21. WILK'S PARK

DIRECTIONS

From central Wagga drive over the Wiradjuri Bridge, after 500 m, turn left at the sweeping bend into Wilk's Park. Note that Wilk's Park is located 300 m from the river. Access to the river is along the walking track past the large Plane Tree adjacent to the Wiradjuri Bridge.

GPS-35.102958 147.372985

The amenities offered at Wilk's Park (toilets, electric barbeque, tables and shade, rubbish bins) are located 300 m from the river. Wilk's Park is a rest stop for travellers towing boats, trailers or caravans. The walking track from Wilk's Park into the adjacent North Wagga Common does not allow vehicle access, but provides access to shore based fishing locations.

ACCESS ROADS	★★★★★
BOAT RAMP	NONE
CAMPING	★★★★
SWIMMING	NONE
SHORE BASED FISHING	NONE
TOILETS	★★★★★
SHADE	★★★★★
BINS	★★★★★
BARBEQUES	★★★★★
TABLES/SEATS	★★★★★

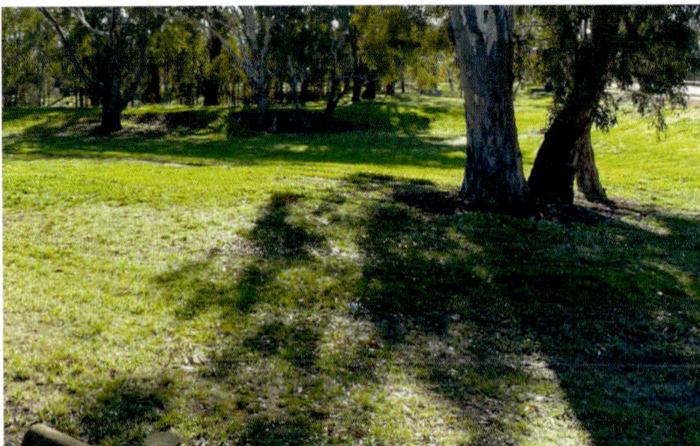

22. NORTH WAGGA COMMON

ACCESS ROADS	★
BOAT RAMP	★★
CAMPING	★
SWIMMING	★★
SHORE BASED FISHING	★★
TOILETS	NONE
SHADE	★★★★
BINS	NONE
BARBEQUES	NONE
TABLES/SEATS	NONE

DIRECTIONS

The North Wagga Common is best accessed 300 m north of the Black Swan Hotel (located on Wall Street) through the white boom gate. Descend down the levy into the Common. Note that there are other steep, rutted entrances to the Common along the levy bank south of the Hotel along Wall Street.

GPS -35.091413 147.373242

North Wagga Common has many 4WD tracks with deep ruts and potholes. 4WD is recommended in wet and dry conditions. The boat ramp is located toward the middle of the common at -35.095130 147.370937. The ramp is concrete and suitable for launching boats during high water periods only, as the ramp is very short. Boat launching at all water levels and weather conditions is available using the concrete boat ramp at Wiradjuri Reserve located on the opposite shore. Note that a 4 knot zone exists in this section of river. North Wagga Common has many tracks along the river bank giving good access to fish habitat. There are few open campsites.

23. WIRADJURI RESERVE

DIRECTIONS

Turn into Narrung Street from Travers Street. Proceed 250 m past Galing Place to the reserve entrance on right.

GPS -35.097668 147.366989

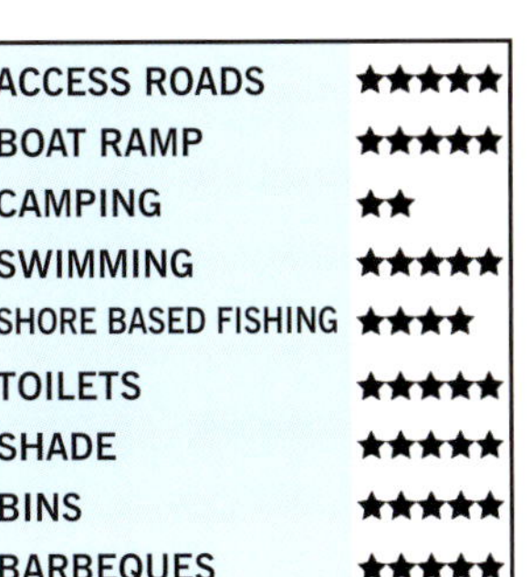

ACCESS ROADS	★★★★★
BOAT RAMP	★★★★★
CAMPING	★★
SWIMMING	★★★★★
SHORE BASED FISHING	★★★★
TOILETS	★★★★★
SHADE	★★★★★
BINS	★★★★★
BARBEQUES	★★★★★
TABLES/SEATS	★★★★

Wiradjuri is one of Wagga's most popular reserves offering excellent swimming off a sand/stony beach and contains the city's main boat ramp. 2WD boat launching is available for boats of all sizes from the high-quality concrete ramp. The reserve contains serviced toilets and barbeque facilities. It's an ideal family reserve with ample frontage to find your own picnic area. The shallow water and slow current make it a particularly good swimming location. Wiradjuri offers a limited number of camp sites as access to many areas is restricted. Boating is popular and care should be taken to avoid shallow water, islands and mid-river snags. A 4 knot zone starts just downstream of the boat ramp. Shore based angling is better above and below the beach (along the walking track).

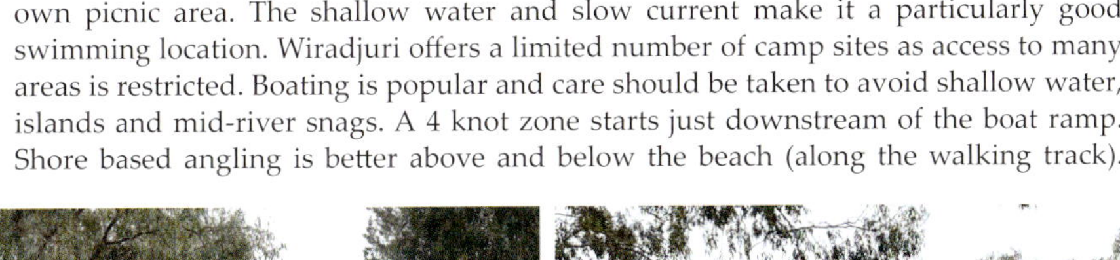

24. GOBBA TSR

DIRECTIONS

Turn from the Old Narrandera Road into River Road. Proceed for 1.2 km and turn left into the reserve.

GPS -35.087147 147.334892

ACCESS ROADS	★★★
BOAT RAMP	★★★
CAMPING	★★★
SWIMMING	★
SHORE BASED FISHING	★★★★
TOILETS	NONE
SHADE	★★★★
BINS	NONE
BARBEQUES	NONE
TABLES/SEATS	NONE

The access road through Gobba TSR is 2WD when dry and 4WD when wet. Boat launching is available at the end of the access road where it loops around adjacent to the river. The launch site is dirt and suitable for 4WD or remote launch. Gobba TSR has many open camp sites under large trees. The bank is steep with the few access points to the water offering good angling.

25. FROG HOLLOW

ACCESS ROADS	★★★★★
BOAT RAMP	NONE
CAMPING	NONE
SWIMMING	NONE
SHORE BASED FISHING	★★★★
TOILETS	NONE
SHADE	★★★★★
BINS	NONE
BARBEQUES	NONE
TABLES/SEATS	NONE

DIRECTIONS

Turn from the Sturt Highway into McNickle Road. Proceed for 1.1 km to gate. Continue straight to the river (do not turn left into private property).

GPS -35.111731 147.323989

Frog Hollow is a small river frontage featured by ease of access and excellent shaded angling. It isn't suited for young children due to the steep bank, deep water and strong current. No boat launching or camping is available at this site.

26. ASHMONT RESERVE

ACCESS ROADS	★★★★
BOAT RAMP	★★★
CAMPING	★★★
SWIMMING	★
SHORE BASED FISHING	★★★★
TOILETS	NONE
SHADE	★★★★
BINS	NONE
BARBEQUES	NONE
TABLES/SEATS	NONE

DIRECTIONS

Turn north from the Sturt Highway into McNickle Road. Proceed for 650 m, then turn left into Roach Road. Continue along Roach Road for 1.8 km to the reserve entrance on the right (note that the boom gate into the reserve is 400 m down this road).

GPS -35.107450 147.308543

The access road to the front gate is 2WD, however the gate is generally locked. Ashmont Reserve is an ideal location to walk in and fish from the shore. Shore based fishing is excellent with numerous angling opportunities along the waterfront. Boats can be launched (when the boom gate is open) from the sloping dirt ramp 200 m along the main track.

27. RIVER ROAD RESERVE

ACCESS ROADS	★★★★
BOAT RAMP	★★★
CAMPING	★
SWIMMING	★
SHORE BASED FISHING	★★★★★
TOILETS	NONE
SHADE	★★
BINS	NONE
BARBEQUES	NONE
TABLES/SEATS	NONE

DIRECTIONS

The gate into River Road Reserve is located 4.5 km from the Old Narrandera Road to the east and 2.5 km from the Old Narrandera Road to the west (note that River Road is looped, with eastern and western entrances to the Old Narrandera Road).

GPS-35.077560 147.303441

Access into this small reserve is 2WD all weather. Boat launching is 4WD or remote launch. This reserve is featured by the steep clay drop-off and large eddy along the waterfront creating excellent shore based angling. The fishing ledge is suitable for several anglers. Camping is available on top of the bank, which is an open area with little shade.

28. YARRAGUNDRY TSR (ARMSTRONG'S)

DIRECTIONS

Turn right from the Sturt Highway into Armstrongs Road (1.7 km east of 11 Mile Road and 1.1 km west of Yarragundry Road). Proceed along the dirt track for 1.2 km to reserve. Note that the road across the bridge leads into private property.

GPS-35.108548 147.214836

ACCESS ROADS	★★★★★
BOAT RAMP	★★★★
CAMPING	★★★★
SWIMMING	★
SHORE BASED FISHING	★★★★
TOILETS	NONE
SHADE	★★★
BINS	NONE
BARBEQUES	NONE
TABLES/SEATS	NONE

Yarragundry TSR (commonly known as Armstrong's) is readily accessible to 2WD and large boats can be launched from the trailer using the well-formed dirt ramp. Yarragundry TSR has good camping with large red gums providing shade. Shore based fishing is excellent. Navigation in this area is good with relatively few mid-river snags.

29. MILLERS LANE RESERVE

DIRECTIONS

Turn south from the Old Narrandera Road into O'Sheas Road. Follow O'Sheas Road for 3.0 km and then turn right into Millers Lane. Continue along Millers Lane and turn right through the rusted double gates immediately before the cattle grid. Follow the track adjacent to the fence to the river.

GPS -35.086105 147.215159

ACCESS ROADS	★★★★
BOAT RAMP	NONE
CAMPING	★★★
SWIMMING	NONE
SHORE BASED FISHING	★★★★
TOILETS	NONE
SHADE	★★
BINS	NONE
BARBEQUES	★★
TABLES/SEATS	NONE

Millers Lane is a neat, clean reserve situated high above a sweeping bend in the river. Access to the water is restricted by a fence along the steep cliff. Water access is possible, but difficult. There are several small locations for shore based fishing. Millers Lane has open, flat areas for camping and caravans. The tracks are 2WD when dry, but slippery when wet. No boat launching is available.

30. KOHLHAGEN'S BEACH

ACCESS ROADS	★★★★★
BOAT RAMP	★★★
CAMPING	★★★★★
SWIMMING	★★★★★
SHORE BASED FISHING	★★★
TOILETS	NONE
SHADE	★★★★
BINS	NONE
BARBEQUES	NONE
TABLES/SEATS	NONE

DIRECTIONS

Turn from the Sturt Highway into Kohlhagen's Road (800 m east of 12 Mile Road, 1.2 km west of 11 Mile Road). Proceed for 2 km along the dirt road to the reserve.

GPS -35.104375 147.184623

Kohlhagen's Beach is a popular reserve for swimming, fishing and boating. The access road is all weather 2WD. The best launch sites (for all sized boats) are located at the lower and upper ends of the beach (4WD is recommended). Swimming is ideal with shallow water and slow current. Kohlhagen's offers good camping with better shade at the western end of the reserve. Shore based fishing is poor off the beach itself, however at either end of the beach where the water deepens, angling is good.

REGION OVERVIEW
MAP 5 - CURRAWARNA

BALRANALD
MAUDE
HAY
UARDRY
CARRATHOOL
YARADDA / BENEREMBAH
DARLINGTON POINT
YANCO
NARRANDERA
GALORE
MAP 5
CURRAWARNA
WAGGA WAGGA
OURA
WANTABADGERY
GUNDAGAI

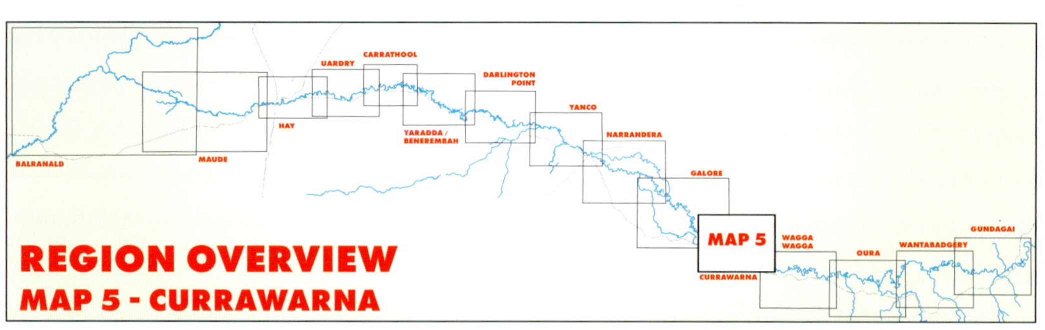

Lower Middle Road
The Bulls Run
Roping Pole Road
JONES RESERVE
38
Rands Tank Road
Ganmurra Road
River
Murrumbidgee
Old Narrandera Road
Gap Road
Brushwood Road
Old Man Creek
40
Central Island Road
CENTRAL ISLAND ROAD, OLD MAN CREEK
LEITCH RESERVE, OLD MAN CREEK
Ganmurra Road
CURRAWANANNA STATE FOREST (WEST)
To Galore
To Narrandera
Leitch Road
37
Kerfoot Road
36
Bidgee Street
35
Bullenbung Creek Bridge
39
BULLENBUNG CREEK BRIDGE, OLD MAN CREEK
Central Island Rd
Old Man Creek
Bullenbung Creek
STURT HIGHWAY
CURRAWANANNA STATE FOREST
Rohans Road
Old Man Creek
34
MURRUMBIDGEE VALLEY NATIONAL PARK (BERRY JERRY), OLD MAN CREEK
33
N
NE
E
SE
S
SW
W
NW
Bunyon's Road
Cameron's Road
0
1
2
3
4
5
Kilometres

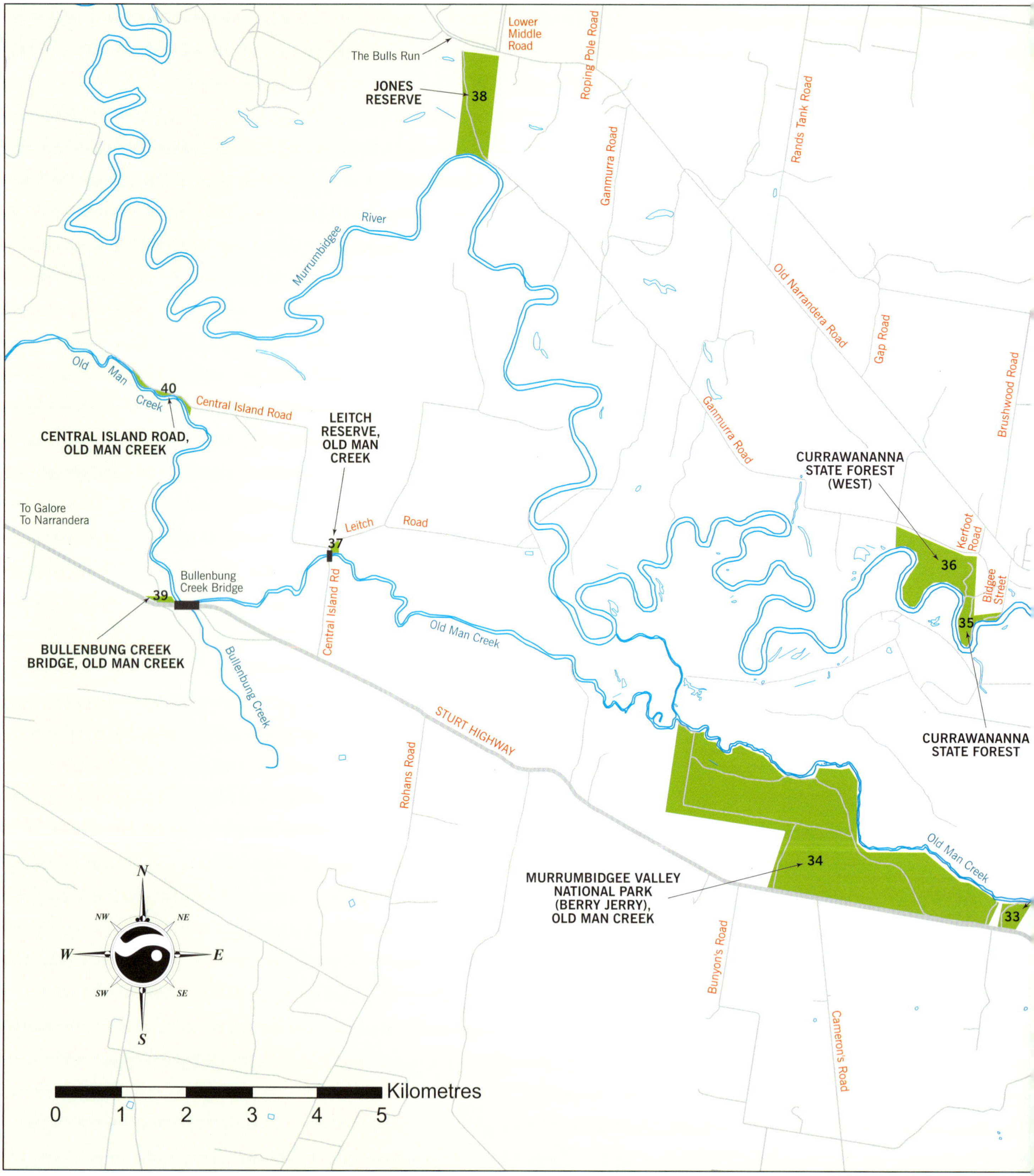

CURRAWARNA REGION

To Coolamon
Cleek Street
Cottee Road
Jenkins Road
Millwood Road
East Millwood Road
AWARNA
rrumbidgee River
Mundowey Bridge
Old Narrandera Road
Berry Jerry Lane
31
KOHLHAGEN'S TSR (17 MILE)
OLD MAN CREEK BRIDGE (BEAVERS CREEK WEIR)
32
Boytons Road
Mundowy Lane
Collingullie
To Lockhart
To The Rock
To Wagga

The Currawarna region is where the Old Man Creek diverges from the Murrumbidgee River. The Creek is a permanent waterway which meanders through prime farmland before re-entering the river approximately 70 km downstream. The Old Narrandera road on the northern bank and the Sturt Highway on the southern bank are linked by bridges across the River and Creek giving access to reserves on both waterways. The river through Currawarna and downstream offers some of the best low water navigation and the size of the reserves offer isolated campsites. The Old Man Creek is a typically narrow and snag filled, making boat navigation difficult at times, but the shore based fishing is excellent.

31. KOHLHAGEN'S TSR (17 MILE)

DIRECTIONS

The entrance to the reserve is located off the Old Narrandera Road, 100 m east of Millwood Road.

GPS -35.031303 147.143877

ACCESS ROADS	★★★
BOAT RAMP	★★★
CAMPING	★★★★
SWIMMING	★★★
SHORE BASED FISHING	★★★★
TOILETS	NONE
SHADE	★★★★★
BINS	NONE
BARBEQUES	NONE
TABLES/SEATS	NONE

Kohlhagen's TSR (commonly known as 17 Mile) is a large reserve with moderate 2WD access. The roads are slippery and when wet restricting travel to 4WD. The large size of the reserve creates many excellent campsites, particularly toward the western boundary. Steep banks for much of the waterfront restrict boat launching to a single site located immediately downstream of the steep cliff (veer right from the main track 1.6 km from the gate). The dirt ramp is suitable to launch trailer boats using 4WD or remote-launch. A narrow track follows the waterfront providing access to numerous fishing and camping locations. Boat and shore based fishing is excellent.

32. OLD MAN CREEK BRIDGE (BEAVERS CREEK WEIR)

ACCESS ROADS	★★★★
BOAT RAMP	NONE
CAMPING	★★
SWIMMING	★
SHORE BASED FISHING	★★★★★
TOILETS	NONE
SHADE	★★★
BINS	★
BARBEQUES	NONE
TABLES/SEATS	NONE

DIRECTIONS

Turn north from the Sturt Hwy into Mundowy Lane. Proceed for 2.5 km to the bridge and turn left immediately once over the bridge into the reserve. From the Old Narrandera Road turn south into Mundowy Lane and proceed for 5.2 km to the bridge. Turn right into reserve immediately before the bridge.

GPS -35.061466 147.123616

Old Man Creek Bridge provides access to the excellent shore based fishing provided by the tailrace of Beavers Creek Weir (located 1 km upstream). The reserve area is suitable for caravans with open, flat areas overlooking the water. Note that the reserve has steep access to the shore. No trailer boat launching is available, however canoes and car-toppers can be carried down the steep bank under the bridge. Note that both sides of the creek at the weir are private property.

33. SAWPIT TSR, OLD MAN CREEK

DIRECTIONS

The entrance is 4.6 km west of Mundowy Lane and 1.3 km east of Berry Jerry rest area.

GPS -35.064531 147.067523

ACCESS ROADS	★★★★
BOAT RAMP	★
CAMPING	★★★★★
SWIMMING	★★
SHORE BASED FISHING	★★★★★
TOILETS	NONE
SHADE	★★★★
BINS	NONE
BARBEQUES	NONE
TABLES/SEATS	NONE

Sawpit TSR provides easy access to the Old Man Creek immediately upstream of Murrumbidgee Valley National Park (Berry Jerry). The road through this reserve is suitable for 2WD. In wet weather the track is slippery, requiring 4WD. Boat launching is limited to remote-launch from an area alongside the western boundary fence. The Old Man Creek has many boating hazards due to snags and shallow water; however this reserve offers approximately one kilometre of open water. The foreshore is ideal for angling with easy access to the water's edge. Excellent camping is available with open spaces and good shade.

34. MURRUMBIDGEE VALLEY NATIONAL PARK (BERRY JERRY), OLD MAN CREEK

ACCESS ROADS	★★★
BOAT RAMP	★★
CAMPING	★★★★★
SWIMMING	★★
SHORE BASED FISHING	★★★
TOILETS	★★★★★
SHADE	★★★★★
BINS	★★★★★
BARBEQUES	NONE
TABLES/SEATS	★★★★★

DIRECTIONS

Turn from the Sturt Highway at the Berry Jerry Rest Area, 8.1 km west of Collingullie.

GPS -35.062296 147.053015

Murrumbidgee Valley National Park (Berry Jerry), on the Old Man Creek, is a large area offering excellent camping and fishing. Access roads are 2WD when dry and 4WD when wet. The entrance to Berry Jerry has a rest area with toilets, tables and chairs, parking and rubbish bins. Once inside the National Park, there are no facilities. The road from the entrance to the western boundary is 6.5 km, whilst the road from the entrance to the eastern boundary is 1.5 km. The eastern road follows the fence line and offers boat launching (alongside the boundary) using 4WD or remote launch. The track leading west from the entrance has many secondary tracks that lead to numerous camping and fishing sites sites.

35. CURRAWANANNA STATE FOREST

ACCESS ROADS	★★
BOAT RAMP	★★★
CAMPING	★★★★
SWIMMING	★★★★
SHORE BASED FISHING	★★★
TOILETS	NONE
SHADE	★★★★★
BINS	NONE
BARBEQUES	NONE
TABLES/SEATS	NONE

DIRECTIONS

Turn south from the Old Narrandera Road into Bidgee St (at the Currawarna Community Centre). Turn right into Reserve Road, proceed for 200 m then follow track to the left. Proceed through two sets of gates and over grid to reserve. Take left hand track to boat launch and camp site. The right hand track is unsuitable for vehicles towing (note that this track eventually joins the main camping area and boat launch).

GPS -35.019734 147.065063

Currawananna State Forest is a large area, but has limited river access. The access track is rough and unsuitable for 2WD. Boat launching is 4WD or remote launch at the downstream end of the main beach area. Camping is available at the boat ramp where swimming is also excellent. Shore based fishing is best upstream and downstream of the beach. The right hand track from the grid provides access to many excellent shore based fishing locations.

36. CURRAWANANNA STATE FOREST (WEST)

DIRECTIONS

Turn south from the Old Narrandera Road into Kerfoot Road. Proceed for 600 m then veer left to entrance grid.

GPS -35.014559 147.060280

ACCESS ROADS	★★★
BOAT RAMP	★★★
CAMPING	★★★★
SWIMMING	★★
SHORE BASED FISHING	★★★★
TOILETS	NONE
SHADE	★★★★
BINS	NONE
BARBEQUES	NONE
TABLES/SEATS	NONE

Currawananna State Forest (west) has a range of open, flat camp sites and multiple shore based fishing locations. The access tracks are 2WD when dry, but 4WD when wet. The boat ramp is accessed by turning right 500 m along the main track from the entrance. Continuing along the main track (i.e. following the river, rather than turning right to the boat ramp), provides access to many camping, swimming and fishing locations. Note that this track loops back to the boat ramp area. The dirt ramp is suitable for 4WD or remote launch.

37. LEITCH RESERVE, OLD MAN CREEK

ACCESS ROADS	★★★★
BOAT RAMP	NONE
CAMPING	★★★
SWIMMING	★
SHORE BASED FISHING	★★★★
TOILETS	NONE
SHADE	★★★★
BINS	NONE
BARBEQUES	★★
TABLES/SEATS	NONE

DIRECTIONS

Turn north from the Sturt Highway into Central Island Road. Proceed for 1.6 km, pass over the Bulgary Bridge and then turn right 100 m into Leitch Road, then right again after 100 m into the reserve.

GPS -35.013247 146.955335

Leitch Reserve is a small area adjacent to the Bulgary Bridge. Steep banks prevent trailer boat launching at this site. Car-topper and canoe launching is difficult, but achievable. Camping is good but space is limited. Shore based fishing is excellent with numerous snags along the waterfront.

38. JONES RESERVE

ACCESS ROADS	★★★★
BOAT RAMP	★★★★
CAMPING	★★★
SWIMMING	★
SHORE BASED FISHING	★★★★
TOILETS	NONE
SHADE	★★★★
BINS	NONE
BARBEQUES	NONE
TABLES/SEATS	NONE

DIRECTIONS

Turn into Ganmurra Rd from the Old Narrandera Rd (8.2 km from Kerfoot Rd, Currawarna). Proceed for 2.5 km and turn right at the T intersection. Drive for 2.0 km then proceed through the double gates into the reserve. A second entrance is accessed from the Old Narrandera Rd, 400 m west of Lower Middle Rd and 400 m east of 'The Bulls Run' property sign.

GPS -34.963901 146.984416

Jones Reserve is popular with boat and shore based anglers. The river here is navigable for many kilometres upstream and downstream. Road access is 2WD when dry, however it is slippery when wet requiring 4WD. The boat ramp is located 300 m through the double gates. Boat launching for large boats is available at all water levels with 4WD or remote launch. Camping is good with open space and shade. Shore based angling is excellent along the foreshore with submerged snags creating ideal habitat. Additional camp sites and shore based fishing opportunities are accessed through the single gate at the western end of the reserve.

39. BULLENBUNG CREEK BRIDGE, OLD MAN CREEK

DIRECTIONS

Turn north from the Sturt Highway, 100 m west of the Bullenbung Bridge. Proceed along the track parallel to the Highway toward the bridge.

GPS -35.021672 146.926982

ACCESS ROADS	★★★★
BOAT RAMP	★
CAMPING	★★★
SWIMMING	★
SHORE BASED FISHING	★★★★
TOILETS	NONE
SHADE	★★★★
BINS	NONE
BARBEQUES	NONE
TABLES/SEATS	NONE

This small reserve is located at the junction of Bullenbung Creek and Old Man Creek. These creeks converge underneath the bridge where mixing of the two water bodies creates excellent angling opportunities. Boat launching is unavailable during low water levels, but in high flows the gravel ramp beside the bridge provides 4WD or remote launch. Camping is good with flat sites on top of the bank below shady trees. The access roads are 2WD in all weather.

CARRATHOOL
UARDRY
DARLINGTON POINT
HAY
YANCO
YARADDA / BENEREMBAH
NARRANDERA
BALRANALD
MAUDE
GALORE
MAP 6
WAGGA WAGGA
GUNDAGAI
OURA
WANTABADGERY
CURRAWARNA
REGION OVERVIEW
MAP 6 - GALORE

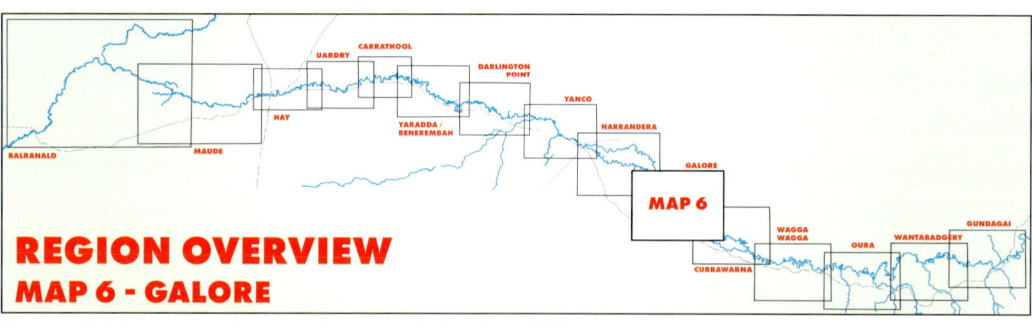

49
OLD MAN CREEK LANE
Berembed Weir Sign
Slatteries Road
Deepwater Matong Road
Bundigerry Canal
Berembed Weir Road
Brewaranna Lane
BEREMBED WEIR (NORTH)
44
BUNDIGERRY CREEK OFFTAKE (BUNDIGERRY CANAL)
46
45
Murrumbidgee River
BEREMBED WEIR (SOUTH)
Old Man Creek
43
PIPERS RESERVE
McKenzies Road
Central Island Road
To Narrandera
Weir Road
42
GALORE BRIDGE, OLD MAN CREEK
STURT HIGHWAY
40
CENTRAL ISLAND ROAD, OLD MAN CREEK
41
LENEHANS TSR, OLD MAN CREEK
BULLENBUNG CREEK BRIDGE, OLD MAN CREEK
GALORE
Kings Road
Arajoel Road
(entrance is 400m before apex of corner)
39
To Collingullie

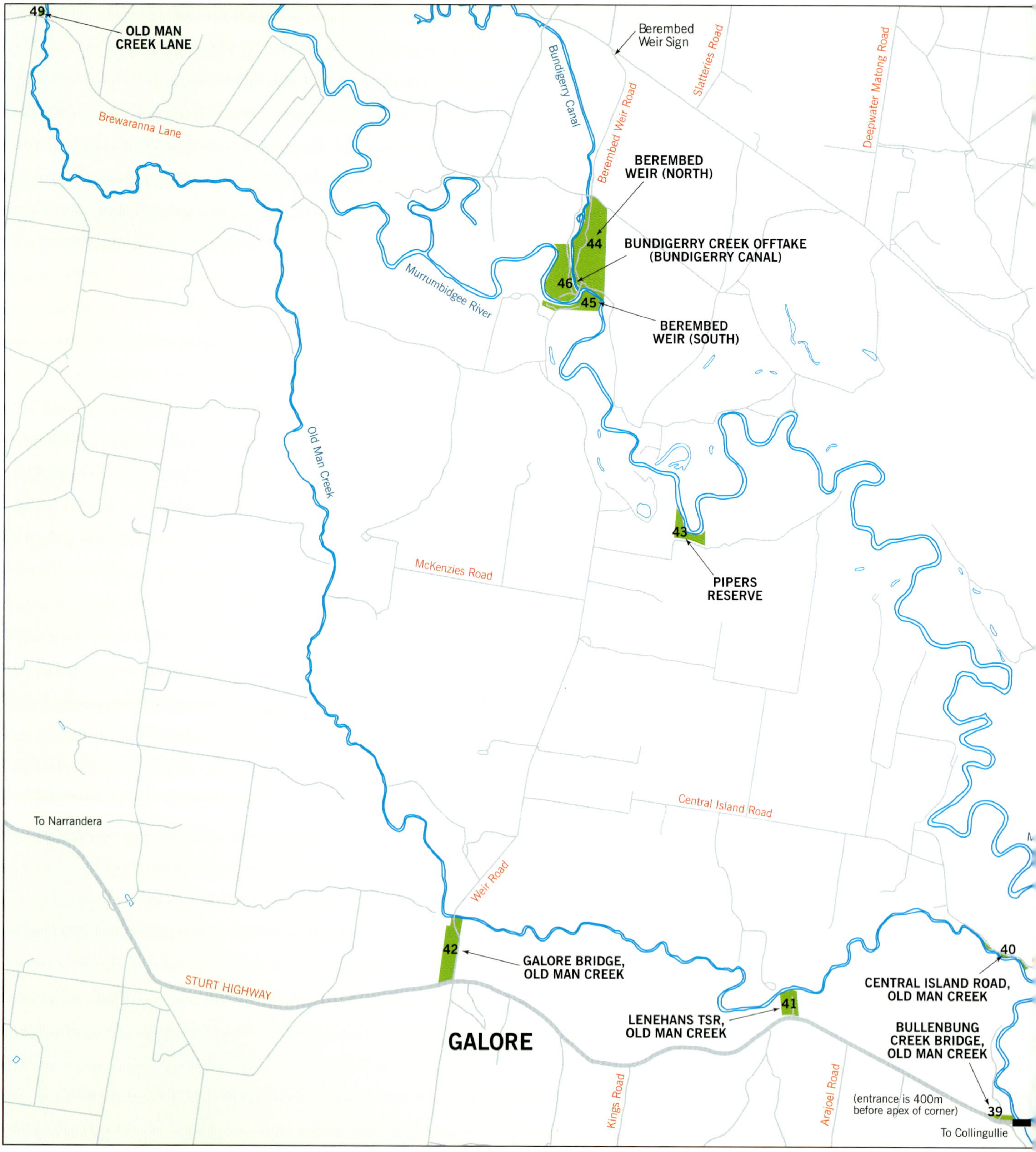

GALORE REGION

Galore gained its name from an early explorer who crested the top of Galore Hill and noted to his companion that there was 'green grass galore'. Apart from the isolated mount of Galore Hill, this area is essentially flat grazing and cropping land. Accordingly the river is slow, deep, wide and meandering. Like Currawarna upstream, the Galore area offers access to both the Old Man Creek and the Murrumbidgee River, but it's the weir at Berembed which is the feature of this region. Water from the weir is diverted to the Murrumbidgee Irrigation Area via the man made Bundigerry Canal offering a variety of fishing habitat both above and below the weir.

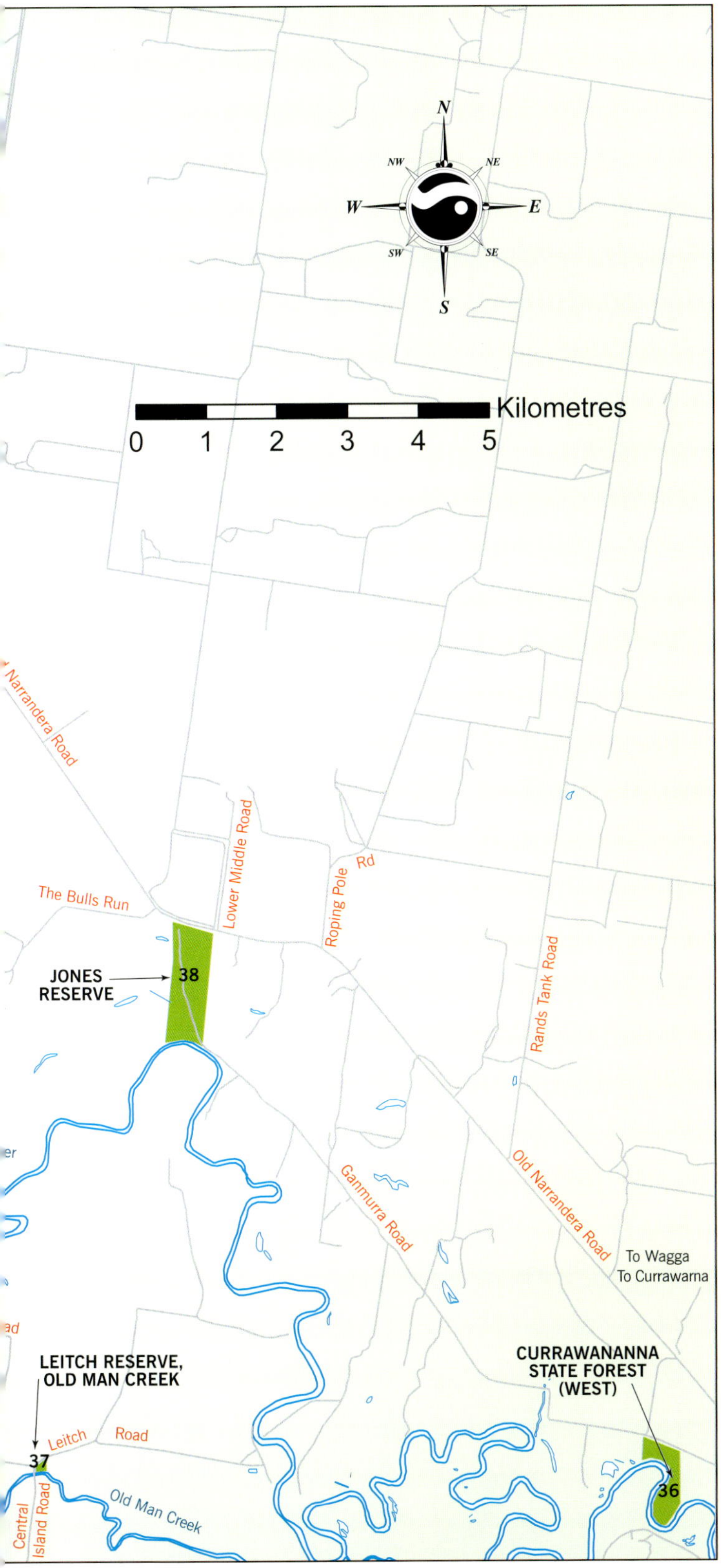

N
NW
NE
W
E
SW
SE
S
Kilometres
0 1 2 3 4 5
Narrandera Road
Lower Middle Road
Roping Pole Rd
The Bulls Run
JONES RESERVE
38
Rands Tank Road
Ganmurra Road
Old Narrandera Road
To Wagga
To Currawarna
LEITCH RESERVE, OLD MAN CREEK
CURRAWANANNA STATE FOREST (WEST)
Leitch Road
37
36
Old Man Creek
Central Island Road

40. CENTRAL ISLAND ROAD, OLD MAN CREEK

ACCESS ROADS	★★★★
BOAT RAMP	NONE
CAMPING	★★★★
SWIMMING	★
SHORE BASED FISHING	★★★★
TOILETS	NONE
SHADE	★★★★
BINS	NONE
BARBEQUES	NONE
TABLES/SEATS	NONE

DIRECTIONS

Turn north from the Sturt Highway into Central Island Road. Proceed for 5 km to the start of the easement on the left.

GPS -34.994401 146.930973

Central Island Road is a long, thin easement between Central Island Road and the Old Man Creek. At approximately 100 m wide (in parts) and 1 km long, this area offers excellent camping under shady trees. Boat launching is restricted to car-toppers and canoes because of steep banks. Access is excellent along the groomed Central Island Road. This section of the Old Man Creek has good fish habitat and accordingly shore based fishing is excellent.

ACCESS ROADS	★★★★
BOAT RAMP	★★
CAMPING	★★★
SWIMMING	★
SHORE BASED FISHING	★★★★
TOILETS	NONE
SHADE	★★★
BINS	NONE
BARBEQUES	NONE
TABLES/SEATS	NONE

41. LENEHAN'S TSR, OLD MAN CREEK

DIRECTIONS

The entrance is 3.6 km east of Kings Road and 750 m west of Arajoel Road. The gate is located 300 m along the track that runs parallel to the Sturt Highway. This side track is accessed opposite the red brick electricity sub-station (located in the paddock south of the highway).

GPS -35.003858 146.882474

Lenehan's TSR is 2WD accessible and suitable for caravans. The track is slippery when wet. Launching of trailer boats is possible down the sloping bank beside the western boundary fence. This launch site requires 4WD or remote-launch. Navigation in the Old Man Creek is limited in low water as exposed snags limit movement. Lenehan's is an excellent campsite with open spaces and good shade trees. Shore based fishing is excellent with good fish habitat along the foreshore.

42. GALORE BRIDGE, OLD MAN CREEK

DIRECTIONS

Turn north from the Sturt Highway at Galore into Weir Road. Proceed for 1 km. Turn right 100 m before the bridge into the reserve. A second entrance is located 200 m before the bridge.

GPS -34.987746 146.810864

ACCESS ROADS	★★★★
BOAT RAMP	NONE
CAMPING	★★★★
SWIMMING	★
SHORE BASED FISHING	★★★★
TOILETS	NONE
SHADE	★★★★
BINS	NONE
BARBEQUES	NONE
TABLES/SEATS	NONE

The Old Man Creek at Galore Bridge offers open, flat campsites suitable for caravans. The steep bank prevents trailer boat launching. The road to the reserve is bitumen with only a short drive on dirt. Bank fishing is excellent with moderate sloping banks along the foreshore allowing access to a variety of habitats.

43. PIPERS RESERVE

DIRECTIONS

Turn north from the Sturt Highway at Galore into Weir Road. Proceed for 9.0 km and turn right at the superphosphate shed (in paddock on right) into the unnamed entrance lane. Travel along this lane for 1.5 km, then veer left into the reserve. Follow track for approximately 1.0 km to the boat ramp and camping area.

ACCESS ROADS	★★★★
BOAT RAMP	★★★
CAMPING	★★★★★
SWIMMING	★
SHORE BASED FISHING	★★★★
TOILETS	★★★
SHADE	★★★★★
BINS	★★★★
BARBEQUES	NONE
TABLES/SEATS	NONE

GPS -34.924316 146.839703

Pipers Reserve is 2WD accessible in all weather. Pipers provides a dirt ramp that allows trailer boat launching using 4WD and remote-launch. The reserve offers many good campsites with facilities including a toilet and rubbish bins. The river offers excellent angling opportunities along the extensive waterfront. The river at Pipers is generally deep and easily navigable down to Berembed Weir approximately 10 km downstream. Boat fishing is excellent.

44. BEREMBED WEIR (NORTH)

DIRECTIONS

Turn from the Old Narrandera Road into Berembed Weir Road. From the entrance grid, continue for 4.3 km over two further grids. Continue straight once over the final grid, to the picnic area.

ACCESS ROADS	★★★★
BOAT RAMP	★★★
CAMPING	★★★★
SWIMMING	★★
SHORE BASED FISHING	★★★★★
TOILETS	NONE
SHADE	★★★★★
BINS	★★★
BARBEQUES	★★★★★
TABLES/SEATS	★★★★

GPS -34.840423 146.843716

Berembed Weir North has well-groomed access from the Old Narrandera Road to the weir. The weir keeper's house (near the weir wall) is adjacent to a large picnic area that has lawns, tables and chairs, electric barbeques, bins and good shade trees. The picnic area is fenced off with no river access. To access the river, cross the weir wall over the Bundigerry Canal and follow the dirt track along the river edge. This track is 2WD (4WD when wet) and provides access to several open, flat riverside campsites. Trailer boat launching is available 400 m along this track from the canal. This launch site requires a steep descent down the bank to access a beach launch (requires 4WD). The best launch site is located at the downstream extremity of the reserve. To get here, follow the right hand track immediately after crossing the canal. This track is rough and 4WD is recommended. This area offers a reasonable dirt ramp to launch trailer boats. Boat and shore based fishing is excellent in this vicinity.

45. BEREMBED WEIR (SOUTH)

ACCESS ROADS	★★★★
BOAT RAMP	★★
CAMPING	★★★★
SWIMMING	★★
SHORE BASED FISHING	★★★
TOILETS	NONE
SHADE	★★★★★
BINS	NONE
BARBEQUES	NONE
TABLES/SEATS	NONE

DIRECTIONS

Turn north from the Sturt Highway at Galore into Weir Road. Proceed for 13 km to the T intersection. Turn right and follow this road for 1.0 km to the entrance.

GPS -34.884807 146.831511

Berembed Weir South includes areas above and below the weir wall. Access to both areas is on the same 2WD accessible track (4WD when wet). There are limited camp sites below the wall, with the sandy beach area offering an ideal location. Boating and fishing closures exist below the weir. Shore based fishing below the weir is good where the access road first meets the river. Above the weir, willow trees prevent river access in most locations, However, a gap in the willow trees forms the boat ramp, where in high water, trailer boats are launched with 4WD or remote-launch. In low water it's difficult to launch craft other than a car-topper or canoe. Camping above the weir is excellent with ample shade. Shore based angling above the weir is limited due to high banks and dense willow growth. The weir pool offers excellent boat fishing.

46. BUNDIGERRY CREEK OFFTAKE (BUNDIGERRY CANAL)

DIRECTIONS

Turn from the Old Narrandera Road into Berembed Weir Road. From the entrance grid, continue for 4.3 km over two further grids. The Bundigerry Canal and offtake are accessed by taking the track to the right once over the final grid.

GPS -34.840423 146.843716

ACCESS ROADS	★★★★
BOAT RAMP	NONE
CAMPING	★
SWIMMING	NONE
SHORE BASED FISHING	★★★★
TOILETS	NONE
SHADE	★★★
BINS	NONE
BARBEQUES	NONE
TABLES/SEATS	NONE

The Bundigerry Creek offtake (commonly known as Bundigerry Canal) is adjacent to Berembed Weir North and offers good shore based fishing opportunities. The canal banks are steep, however there are a variety of fish habitats (e.g. rocks, clay ledges and eddies) that anglers can access. Swimming and boating in the canal is dangerous due to changing water levels, fast current, sharp rocks and steep banks. Trailer boat launching is not available at this site.

REGION OVERVIEW
MAP 7 - NARRANDERA

BALRANALD
MAUDE
HAY
UARDRY
CARRATHOOL
YARADDA / BENEREMBAH
DARLINGTON POINT
YANCO
NARRANDERA
MAP 7
GALORE
WAGGA WAGGA
CURRAWARNA
OURA
WANTABADGERY
GUNDAGAI

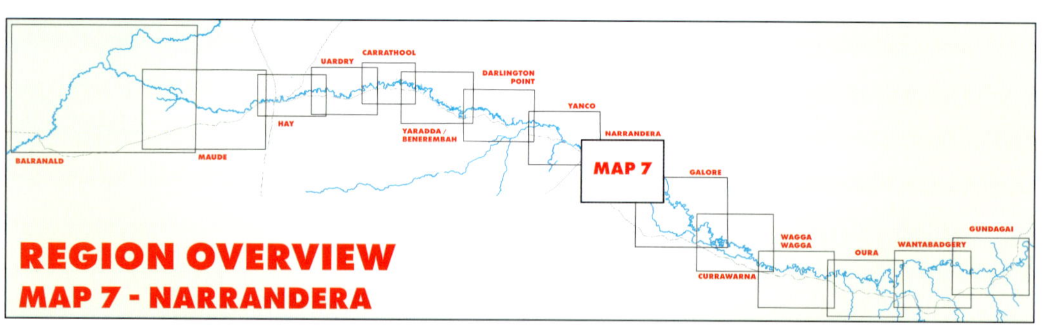

To Leeton
MURRUMBIDGEE VALLEY REGIONAL PARK (NARRANDERA NORTH)
NARRANDERA TOWN BEACH
NARRANDERA
McLays Rd
Irrigation Way
62
63
61
Cadell St
Victoria Ave
Larmer St
Broad St
Lake Talbot
Old Brewery Rd
59
57
LAKE TALBOT, BUNDIGERRY CREEK
ROCKY WATER HOLES, BUNDIGERRY CREEK
56
Old Wagga Road
NEWELL HIGHWAY
FIVE MILE RESERVE, BUNDIGERRY CREEK
55
7 MILE RESERVE, BUNDIGERRY CREEK
53
Old Narrandera Road
Bundigerry Creek
To Hay
Gillenbah
MURRUMBIDGEE VALLEY REGIONAL PARK (NARRANDERA SOUTH)
58
60
NEWELL HIGHWAY
BREWERY FLAT BOAT RAMP
Narrandera Fisheries Centre
To Jerilderie
MILTHORPES TSR
NARRANDERA COMMON
Buckingbong Rd
The Gap Road
54
BUCKINGBONG RESERVE
Murrumbidgee
River
Dellapool Station
OLD MAN CREEK LANE
Brewaranna Lane
Arrambee Road
N
NW
NE
W
E
SW
SE
S
Strontian Road
STURT HIGHWAY
Sandigo River Road
0 1 2 3 4 5
Kilometres
To Collingullie
To Wagga Wagga

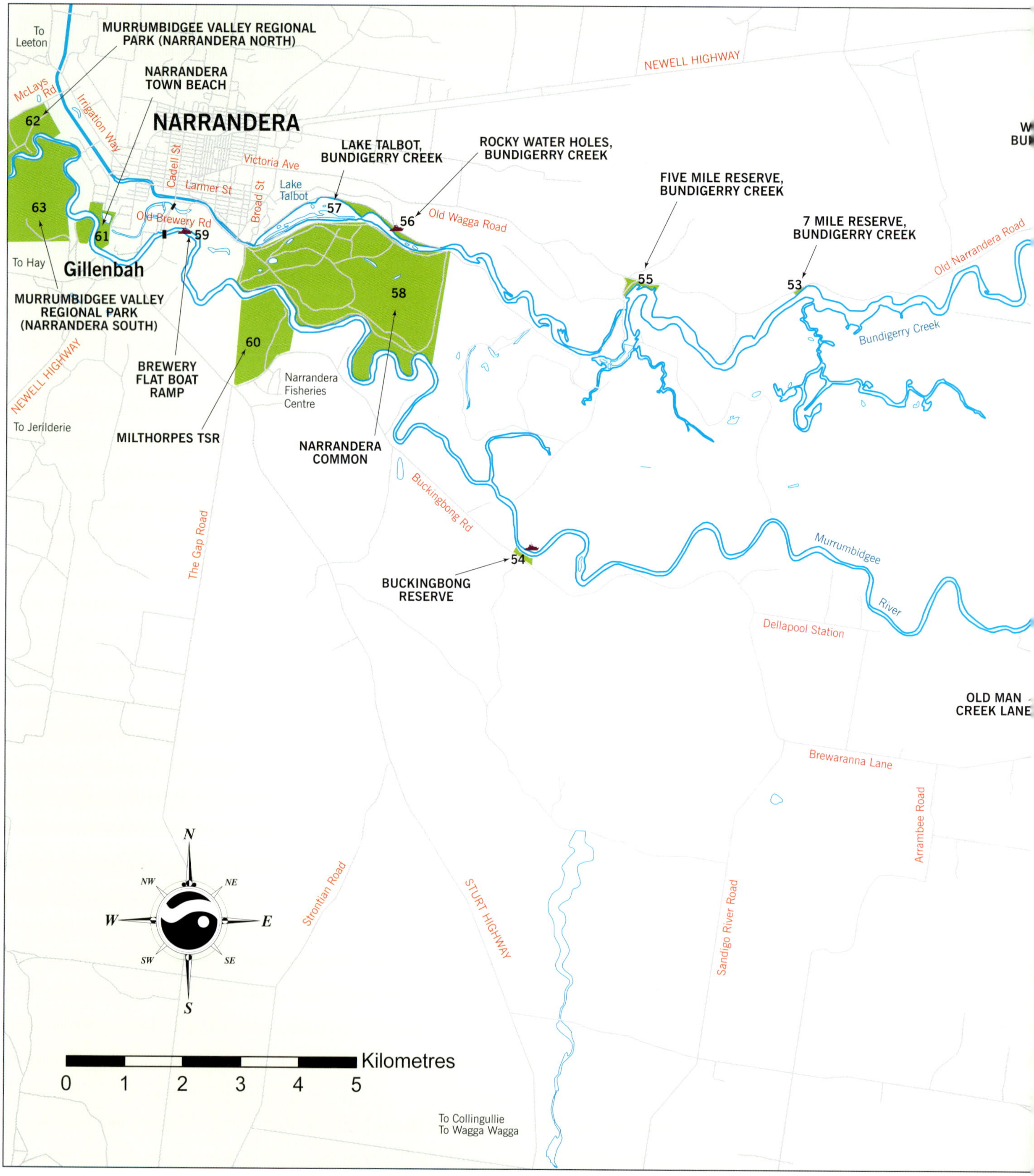

NARRANDERA REGION

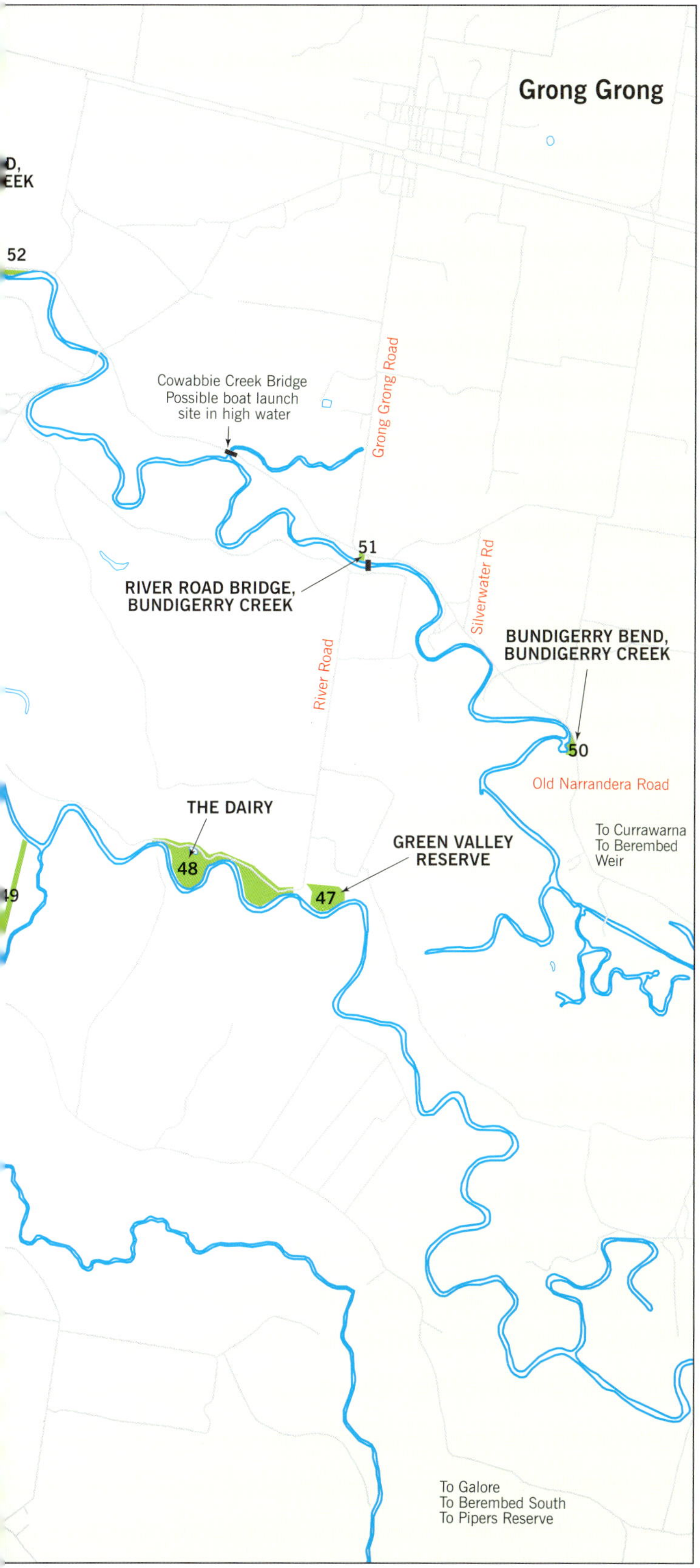

Grong Grong

D,
EEK

52

Cowabbie Creek Bridge
Possible boat launch
site in high water

Grong Grong Road

51

RIVER ROAD BRIDGE,
BUNDIGERRY CREEK

Silverwater Rd

BUNDIGERRY BEND,
BUNDIGERRY CREEK

River Road

50

Old Narrandera Road

THE DAIRY

GREEN VALLEY
RESERVE

To Currawarna
To Berembed
Weir

48

47

49

To Galore
To Berembed South
To Pipers Reserve

Charles Sturt passed through the Narrandera region on his exploration of the Murrumbidgee and Murray Rivers in 1829. The town grew as a crossing point over the river for people to access the Victorian Goldfields from the north and is an important link to the Murrumbidgee Irrigation Area. Narrandera with its population of 4,000 is a rural town with historic charm. It offers two excellent boat ramps on the Murrumbidgee and a further three on the Bundigerry Creek at Five Mile Reserve, Rocky Water Holes and Lake Talbot. The Murrumbidgee, Old Man Creek and Bundigerry Creek are all accessible in this region giving access to a wide variety of riverine habitat.

47. GREEN VALLEY RESERVE

ACCESS ROADS	★★★★
BOAT RAMP	NONE
CAMPING	★★★★
SWIMMING	★
SHORE BASED FISHING	★★★
TOILETS	NONE
SHADE	★★★★
BINS	NONE
BARBEQUES	NONE
TABLES/SEATS	NONE

DIRECTIONS

Turn from the Old Narrandera Road into River Road at the Bundigerry Creek Bridge. Proceed along River Road for 4.5 km. The entrance is located 100 m from the end of River Road on the left.

GPS -34.822170 146.766772

Green Valley offers good camping on a high bank overlooking the river. Trailer boat launching is not available; however car-toppers and canoes may be carried down the bank. The reserve is 2WD, but slippery when wet. Shore based fishing is reasonable with access to fish habitat along the length of the reserve. The main campsite is located toward the middle of the reserve, whilst a secondary track leads to a good angling bank at the upstream boundary. Note that boats may be launched at 'The Dairy', which is located further downstream.

48. THE DAIRY

ACCESS ROADS	★★★
BOAT RAMP	★★★★
CAMPING	★★★★
SWIMMING	★★
SHORE BASED FISHING	★★★★★
TOILETS	NONE
SHADE	★★★★★
BINS	NONE
BARBEQUES	NONE
TABLES/SEATS	NONE

DIRECTIONS

Turn from the Old Narrandera Road into River Road at the Bundigerry Creek Bridge. Proceed along River Road for 4.6 km. The entrance is located at the end of River Road on the right.

GPS-34.822810 146.766317

The Dairy is a public access road through private property offering several river access points. 4WD activity has created deep holes and ruts, however access is 2WD when dry. A small levee separates private property from the track, so ensure travel is on the river side of the levee. Boat launching is best at the quality dirt ramp 800 m from the entrance gate (turn left off the main track). At this ramp, trailer boats can be launched using 4WD or remote launch. The second launch site is 4.8 km from the entrance gate along the levee track (through two gates). This boat ramp requires a descent down the bank to the clay ledge below, where boats can be launched at all water levels. There are numerous open, flat camp sites in this region. Boat and shore based fishing is excellent.

49. OLD MAN CREEK LANE

ACCESS ROADS	★★
BOAT RAMP	NONE
CAMPING	★★★
SWIMMING	★
SHORE BASED FISHING	★★★
TOILETS	NONE
SHADE	★★★★
BINS	NONE
BARBEQUES	NONE
TABLES/SEATS	NONE

DIRECTIONS

The entrance is to the left of the white gates into Brewarrana Station (100 m west of the Old Man Creek Bridge). Continue for 2.0 km to the river.

GPS -34.834331 146.721826

Old Man Creek Lane is a small reserve with limited access to the river due to the steep bank along the waterfront. The high bank prevents trailer boat launching. The access road is 4WD when wet. The campsite is good with flat, open areas and large, shady trees. Shore based angling is excellent with ideal habitat along the shoreline.

50. BUNDIGERRY BEND, BUNDIGERRY CREEK

ACCESS ROADS	★★★★
BOAT RAMP	NONE
CAMPING	★★★
SWIMMING	★
SHORE BASED FISHING	★★★★
TOILETS	NONE
SHADE	★★★★
BINS	NONE
BARBEQUES	NONE
TABLES/SEATS	NONE

DIRECTIONS

The entrance is 6 km west of Berembed Weir Road and 2 km east of Silverwater Road.

GPS -34.805900 146.8044086

Bundigerry Bend is a small reserve with the entrance hidden 50 m from the Old Narrandera Road. Access is 2WD all weather. Trailer boat launching is not available. Shore based fishing is excellent with snags along the waterfront. Camping is good, but space is limited.

51. RIVER ROAD BRIDGE, BUNDIGERRY CREEK

ACCESS ROADS	★★★★
BOAT RAMP	★★
CAMPING	★★★
SWIMMING	★
SHORE BASED FISHING	★★★
TOILETS	NONE
SHADE	★★★★
BINS	★★★★
BARBEQUES	NONE
TABLES/SEATS	NONE

DIRECTIONS

The reserve is 9.9 km west of Berembed Weir Road and 2.1 km east of the Cowabbie Creek Bridge.

GPS -34.785959 146.775478

Located adjacent to the Old Narrandera Road, River Road Bridge offers good camping (particularly downstream of the boat ramp) and 2WD access. Trailer boat launching is provided by a dirt ramp located 100 m downstream of the bridge. Shore based fishing is good with a long waterfront providing access to excellent habitat. Boat fishing is good in this region with submerged snags and deep water sections.

52. WINDMILL BEND, BUNDIGERRY CREEK

ACCESS ROADS	★★★★★
BOAT RAMP	★★★
CAMPING	★★★
SWIMMING	★
SHORE BASED FISHING	★★★★
TOILETS	NONE
SHADE	★★★
BINS	NONE
BARBEQUES	NONE
TABLES/SEATS	NONE

DIRECTIONS

The reserve is 3.3 km west of Cowabbie Creek Bridge and 9 km east of Five Mile Reserve.

GPS -34.753981 146.732612

Windmill Bend is a long, thin easement between the Old Narrandera Road and Bundigerry Creek. This site is easily accessed with 2WD all weather. Boat launching is 4WD or remote-launch at numerous locations around the sweeping bend. The best camping and boat launching sites are located at the upstream and downstream boundaries. Shore based fishing is excellent with the foreshore readily accessible.

53. 7 MILE RESERVE, BUNDIGERRY CREEK

DIRECTIONS

The entrance is 9.7 km west of Cowabbie Creek Bridge and 3.2 km east of 5 Mile Reserve. Note that a large culvert runs under the Old Narrandera Road 100 m before the eastern boundary of the reserve.

GPS -34.765784 146.667170

ACCESS ROADS	★★★★★
BOAT RAMP	★★★★
CAMPING	★★★
SWIMMING	★
SHORE BASED FISHING	★★★★★
TOILETS	NONE
SHADE	★★★
BINS	NONE
BARBEQUES	NONE
TABLES/SEATS	NONE

7 Mile Reserve features a quality dirt ramp capable of launching trailer boats in all weather. Camping is good with open spaces and shade along the shoreline. Shore based fishing is excellent with access to good habitat along the waterfront. This site is ideal to access the top of the weir pool. Submerged trees create boating hazards and care should be taken. These same snags form excellent fish habitat and as such, boat fishing is excellent.

54. BUCKINGBONG RESERVE

DIRECTIONS

Turn north from the Sturt Highway at the Narrandera Fisheries Centre sign into Buckingbong Road. Proceed past the Narrandera Fisheries Centre for 7 km to the entrance on left.

GPS -34.807614 146.617401

ACCESS ROADS	★★★★★
BOAT RAMP	★★★★★
CAMPING	★★★★
SWIMMING	★★
SHORE BASED FISHING	★★★
TOILETS	★★
SHADE	★★★★
BINS	★★★★★
BARBEQUES	★
TABLES/SEATS	★★★★★

Buckingbong Reserve is easily accessed by 2WD (all weather) and features bitumen road access and a concrete boat ramp. This excellent ramp allows 2WD launching of large boats in all weather and water levels. The reserve features a toilet, fireplace, tables and chairs, rubbish bins and is well maintained by the Narrandera Shire Council. Buckingbong is ideal for family boating with navigable river and good fishing. Camping is good, but tall, steep banks restrict river access. Shore based angling is good, particularly upstream of the boat ramp.

55. FIVE MILE RESERVE, BUNDIGERRY CREEK

DIRECTIONS

The reserve is 12.5 km west of the Cowabbie Creek Bridge and 7.1 km east of the Broad Street and Victoria Avenue intersection at Narrandera.

GPS -34.765460 146.638914

ACCESS ROADS	★★★★★
BOAT RAMP	★★★★★
CAMPING	★★★★★
SWIMMING	★★★★★
SHORE BASED FISHING	★★★
TOILETS	★★
SHADE	★★★★★
BINS	★★★★★
BARBEQUES	NONE
TABLES/SEATS	★★★

Five Mile Reserve is a popular picnic and water skiing area. The access roads are 2WD all weather and a concrete ramp (at the eastern boundary) allows launching of all size boats. The regulator at Five Mile Reserve created a large weir pool stopping current flow. This creates perfect swimming conditions with gently-sloping, sandy shores. Red gums along the edge make a scenic and shady campsite. Facilities include pit toilets, rubbish bins, tables and chairs. Navigation hazards include submerged trees and shallow water areas. Shore based angling is moderate, however boat fishing is excellent.

REGION OVERVIEW
MAP 8 - YANCO
BALRANALD
MAUDE
HAY
UARDRY
CARRATHOOL
YARADDA / BENEREMBAH
DARLINGTON POINT
YANCO
MAP 8
NARRANDERA
GALORE
WAGGA WAGGA
CURRAWARNA
OURA
WANTABADGERY
GUNDAGAI

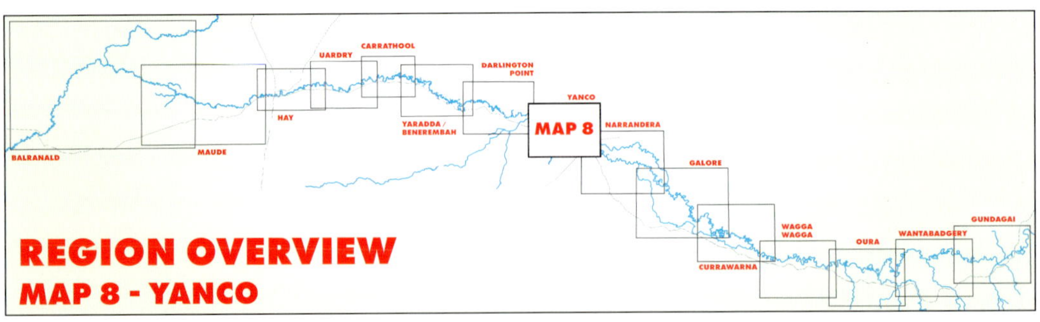

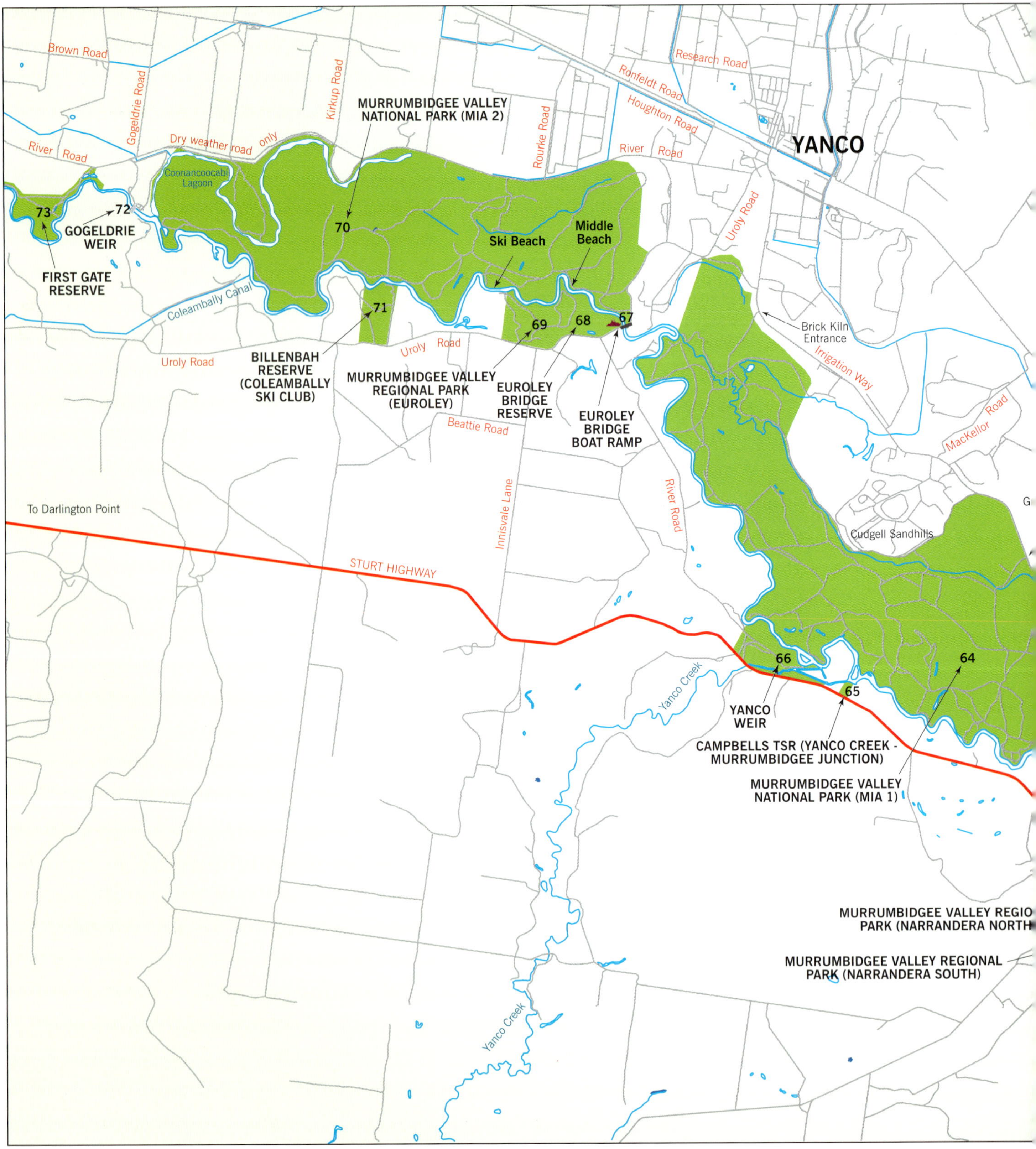

Brown Road
Gogeldrie Road
Kirkup Road
Research Road
Ronfeldt Road
Houghton Road
Rourke Road
MURRUMBIDGEE VALLEY NATIONAL PARK (MIA 2)
YANCO
River Road
Dry weather road only
Coonancoocabil Lagoon
River Road
Uroly Road
73
72
GOGELDRIE WEIR
FIRST GATE RESERVE
70
Ski Beach
Middle Beach
Coleambally Canal
71
69
68
67
Brick Kiln Entrance
Irrigation Way
Uroly Road
Uroly Road
BILLENBAH RESERVE (COLEAMBALLY SKI CLUB)
MURRUMBIDGEE VALLEY REGIONAL PARK (EUROLEY)
EUROLEY BRIDGE RESERVE
EUROLEY BRIDGE BOAT RAMP
MacKellor Road
Beattie Road
Innisvale Lane
River Road
To Darlington Point
Cudgell Sandhills
STURT HIGHWAY
Yanco Creek
66
64
65
YANCO WEIR
CAMPBELLS TSR (YANCO CREEK - MURRUMBIDGEE JUNCTION)
MURRUMBIDGEE VALLEY NATIONAL PARK (MIA 1)
MURRUMBIDGEE VALLEY REGIO PARK (NARRANDERA NORTH
MURRUMBIDGEE VALLEY REGIONAL PARK (NARRANDERA SOUTH)
Yanco Creek

YANCO REGION

The Yanco region derives its name from the local Wiradjuri word interpreted to mean 'the sound of running water'. The region's history since European settlement in the 1840s is closely linked to the development of the Murrumbidgee Irrigation Area (MIA), which started first through private irrigation works before the Government of the day started the MIA project to harness the Murrumbidgee in the early 1900s. The MIA bought the flat, dry plains of the Riverina to life through 2010 km of supply channels, 1391 km of drainage channels servicing some 2500 farms in an area that covers 182,000 hectares. The MIA enabled the subdivision of grazing land into smaller units engaged in mixed farming, dairying, horticulture and sheep-rearing. Italian migrants in the 1950s, drawn by the similarity of soil and climate to Italy, proved vital in the success of local agriculture.

N
NW
NE
W
E
SW
SE
S
Kilometres
0 1 2 3 4 5
Narrandera Airport
Paynters Siding Road
LAKE TALBOT, BUNDIGERRY CREEK
NARRANDERA
Irrigation Way
NEWELL HIGHWAY
ROCKY WATER HOLES, BUNDIGERRY CREEK
Old Wagga Road
62
63
61
59
57
56
58
60
NARRANDERA COMMON
STURT
BREWERY FLAT BOAT RAMP
MILTHORPES TSR
Buckingbong Road
Narrandera Fisheries Centre
The Gap Road
HIGHWAY
NEWELL HIGHWAY
To Jerilderie
To Collingullie
To Wagga

56. ROCKY WATER HOLES, BUNDIGERRY CREEK

DIRECTIONS

The entrance is 2.0 km east of Broad Street along the Old Wagga Road and 17.5 km west of the Cowabbie Creek Bridge.

GPS -34.751100 146.589613

ACCESS ROADS	★★★★★
BOAT RAMP	★★★★★
CAMPING	★★★★
SWIMMING	★★
SHORE BASED FISHING	★★★★★
TOILETS	★★★★★
SHADE	★★★★★
BINS	★★★★★
BARBEQUES	★
TABLES/SEATS	★★★★★

Rocky Water Holes offers excellent camping with flat sites under large red gums. Rocky Water Holes features a sealed access road (down a steep descent), covered tables and chairs, toilet facilities and an all-weather concrete boat ramp. Shored based angling is excellent along the deep waterfront. There are numerous option for boat fishing. A walking track joins Rocky Water Holes to Narrandera township.

57. LAKE TALBOT, BUNDIGERRY CREEK

DIRECTIONS

Turn left from Ngurang Road into Guriyan Road (100 m before the caravan park).

GPS -34.754415 146.567220

ACCESS ROADS	★★★★★
BOAT RAMP	★★★★★
CAMPING	NONE
SWIMMING	NONE
SHORE BASED FISHING	★★★
TOILETS	★★★★★
SHADE	★★★★★
BINS	★★★★★
BARBEQUES	★★★★★
TABLES/SEATS	★★★★★

Lake Talbot is a restricted waterway primarily designed for water skiing. The boom gate opens at 8.00 am and closes at 10.00 pm. The number of boats allowed on the Lake is controlled for safety reasons as the waterway is small. No camping or swimming is allowed, however the site is well serviced with tables and chairs, toilets and rubbish bins, making it ideal for picnics. An additional picnic area is situated at the top of the hill near the entrance gate, which has an electric barbeque, tables, chairs and shade. The access road is bitumen down to the ramp. Shore based fishing is moderate.

58. NARRANDERA COMMON

ACCESS ROADS	★★★★
BOAT RAMP	NONE
CAMPING	★★★
SWIMMING	★★★★★
SHORE BASED FISHING	★★★★
TOILETS	NONE
SHADE	★★★★
BINS	NONE
BARBEQUES	NONE
TABLES/SEATS	★★

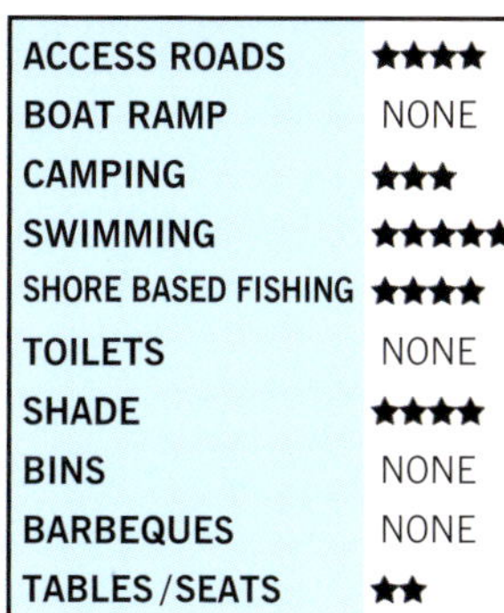

DIRECTIONS

Head south from Narrandera township toward Wagga on the Newell Highway. Cross the bridge over the main canal and turn left into Old Brewery Road. Continue for 1.8 km to the entrance grid.

GPS -34.759193 146.562895

Narrandera Common is a large area between the Main Canal (below Lake Talbot) and the Murrumbidgee River. The track through the Common is approximately 10 km in length. Numerous secondary roads permit access to many kilometres of river frontage and isolated camping and fishing sites. The two beach areas (First Beach at 500 m and Second Beach at 1.4 km from the entrance grid) are signposted and offer excellent swimming and good campsites. The road ends at a nature reserve that has scenic river views and good shore based fishing. Boats are best launched at the Brewery Flat Boat Ramp.

59. BREWERY FLAT BOAT RAMP

ACCESS ROADS	★★★★★
BOAT RAMP	★★★★★
CAMPING	★★★★
SWIMMING	★
SHORE BASED FISHING	★★★
TOILETS	★★★★
SHADE	★★★
BINS	★★★★★
BARBEQUES	★★★★★
TABLES/SEATS	★★★★★

DIRECTIONS

Head south from Narrandera township toward Wagga on the Newell Highway. Cross the bridge over the main canal and turn left into Old Brewery Road. Continue for 200 m to the boat ramp on right.

GPS -34.755963 146.549579

Brewery Flat Boat Ramp is concrete and suitable for launching trailer boats with 2WD. The ramp area has table and chairs, electric barbecue, a shade shelter and a floating pontoon. Adjacent to the ramp is Brewery Flat, which offers open, flat camp sites suitable for vehicles and caravans of all sizes. Brewery Flat also offers serviced toilets.

60. MILTHORPE'S TSR

ACCESS ROADS	★★★★
BOAT RAMP	NONE
CAMPING	★★★
SWIMMING	★★
SHORE BASED FISHING	★★★★
TOILETS	NONE
SHADE	★★★★
BINS	NONE
BARBEQUES	NONE
TABLES/SEATS	NONE

DIRECTIONS

Turn north from the Sturt Highway at the Narrandera Fisheries Centre sign into Buckingbong Road. Proceed for 700 m to the reserve entrance on left (opposite the Narrandera Fisheries Centre).

GPS -34.777571 146.567335

Milthorpe's TSR is a large area that can be accessed by 2WD when dry (4WD when wet). The left fork in the track leads to many shore based fishing locations, and has an excellent, secluded camp site. The right fork leads to a pump house which has an open, flat campsite. This area has steep banks and difficult access to the water. Shore based fishing is good where the river can be accessed.

61. NARRANDERA TOWN BEACH

ACCESS ROADS	★★★
BOAT RAMP	NONE
CAMPING	★★★★
SWIMMING	★★★★★
SHORE BASED FISHING	★
TOILETS	NONE
SHADE	★★★★
BINS	★★★★
BARBEQUES	NONE
TABLES/SEATS	★★

DIRECTIONS

Turn west into Larmer Street from Cadell Street (at Police station) and proceed over the canal bridge. Larmer Street veers left and becomes Townsend Street. Follow this road until it becomes dirt and travel under the railway viaduct to the beach.

GPS -34.755918 146.541857

Town Beach is primarily a swimming area with slow current and shallow water. It's ideal for picnics and family day trips. Boat launching is restricted to car-toppers or canoes as no ramp is available. The access road under the viaduct is 2WD however the reserve has many other tracks which 4WD activity has made unsuitable for low clearance vehicles. Shore based fishing is poor due to the mostly shallow, sandy bottom. Better fishing habitat is located upstream and downstream of the beach. There are many open, flat areas for camping.

62. MURRUMBIDGEE VALLEY REGIONAL PARK (NARRANDERA NORTH)

DIRECTIONS

Turn south from Irrigation Way into McLays Road. Cross the canal and proceed to the Park entrance.

GPS -34.735894 146.530325

ACCESS ROADS	★★★★
BOAT RAMP	★
CAMPING	★★★
SWIMMING	★★★★
SHORE BASED FISHING	★★★
TOILETS	NONE
SHADE	★★★★
BINS	NONE
BARBEQUES	NONE
TABLES/SEATS	NONE

Murrumbidgee Valley Regional Park (Narrandera North) has well-groomed roads that access several camps either from the main track, or using secondary trails. Punt Trail leads to a large beach camp area, which is ideal for swimming and shore based fishing. The main track meanders for approximately 1 km before opening out on a sandy point offering good swimming and shore based fishing. Access through the Regional Park is 2WD in dry weather, but 4WD when wet. Trailer boat launching using 4WD or remote launch is difficult, but possible at the beach areas.

63. MURRUMBIDGEE VALLEY REGIONAL PARK (NARRANDERA SOUTH)

DIRECTIONS

The entrance is 1.1 km west of Gillenbah along the Sturt Highway and 200 m west of the old railway viaduct.

GPS -34.764445 146.531824

ACCESS ROADS	★★★
BOAT RAMP	★
CAMPING	★★★
SWIMMING	★★★★
SHORE BASED FISHING	★★★
TOILETS	NONE
SHADE	★★★★★
BINS	NONE
BARBEQUES	NONE
TABLES/SEATS	NONE

Murrumbidgee Valley Regional Park (Narrandera South) is accessed through Nobles Bend TSR. Together they represent a very large red gum forest. The Regional Park offers several campsites with good shade and sandy beaches. The main road runs parallel to the river looping back toward the entrance. Secondary tracks off this main road access camp sites along the waterfront. These tracks are 4WD and unsuitable for caravans. Trailer boat launching is available across the beaches using 4WD. The waterfront is accessible in many locations offering shore based fishing opportunities, particularly toward the western boundary.

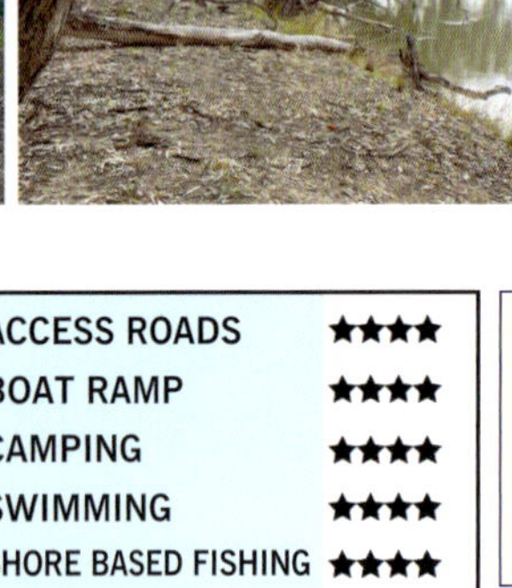

ACCESS ROADS	★★★★
BOAT RAMP	★★★★
CAMPING	★★★★
SWIMMING	★★★★
SHORE BASED FISHING	★★★★
TOILETS	NONE
SHADE	★★★★
BINS	NONE
BARBEQUES	NONE
TABLES/SEATS	NONE

64. MURRUMBIDGEE VALLEY NATIONAL PARK (MIA 1)

DIRECTIONS

The Brick Kiln entrance is 5.3 km west of Mackellar Road and 3.3 km east of Uroly Road. The Graham's Grave entrance is 3.0 km east of Mackellar Road and 6.2 km west of Paynters Siding Road.

GPS -34.685792 146.470410

MIA 1 is a large, forested National Park. Forest Drive is over 20 km from the Brick Kiln entrance to Graham's Grave entrance with numerous secondary tracks leading mainly to beach campsites. The tracks are 2WD when dry, but 4WD in wet weather. The length of the waterfront and ease of access provides numerous opportunities for shore based fishing and secluded camping. Trailer boat launching is available using the concrete boat ramp at Markey's beach. Markey's Beach is best accessed from the Graham's Grave entrance (take Forest Drive from the grid located 2.4 km from the Grahams Grave entrance. Continue right on Forest Drive past Rook Drive and Link Trail, then turn left at the Markey's Beach sign and follow the trail for 1 km to the boat ramp and beach; -34.718691 146.446547). Boat launching is also possible at most beaches using 4WD or remote-launch. MIA 1 encompasses Yanco Weir providing access to the river above and below the weir structure. MIA 1 is ideal for camping or a scenic forest drive.

65. CAMPBELL'S TSR (YANCO CREEK - MURRUMBIDGEE JUNCTION)

ACCESS ROADS	★★★
BOAT RAMP	★★
CAMPING	★★★★
SWIMMING	★
SHORE BASED FISHING	★★★
TOILETS	NONE
SHADE	★★★★★
BINS	NONE
BARBEQUES	NONE
TABLES/SEATS	NONE

DIRECTIONS

The entrance is 12.2 km west of the Newell Highway and Sturt Highway junction (i.e. the Jerilderie turnoff at Gillenbah) and 2.8 km east of the Yanco Weir turnoff.

GPS -34.713718 146.426867

Campbells TSR provides access to the junction of Yanco Creek and the Murrumbidgee River. The reserve has two main camp sites under a red gum canopy. The access track is 4WD and not suited to caravans. Trailer boat launching is available into Yanco Creek using 4WD or remote-launch. Boat launching is difficult during low water levels. Boat fishing is available in both the creek and river. Shore based fishing is good during high flows with easy access along the limited waterfront.

66. YANCO WEIR

ACCESS ROADS	★★★
BOAT RAMP	NONE
CAMPING	★★★
SWIMMING	★
SHORE BASED FISHING	★★★
TOILETS	NONE
SHADE	★★★★★
BINS	★
BARBEQUES	NONE
TABLES/SEATS	NONE

DIRECTIONS

The entrance is 15 km west of the Newell Highway and Sturt Highway junction (i.e. the Jerilderie turnoff at Gillenbah) and 5.9 km east of Innisvale Lane. Turn at the Yanco Weir sign, proceed down River Road for 500 m, then turn right into Yanco Weir Road.

GPS -34.701123 146.402476

Yanco Weir offers a variety of fishing and camping options both above and below the weir. However, there are no boat launching opportunities at either area. Below the weir there are flat, open areas for camping along Yanco Creek. Access to the river below the weir is limited. The area above the weir can be accessed using the right hand track as you approach the boom gate. This track runs parallel to Yanco Creek. Caution should be taken in wet weather as this track becomes slippery. The heavily wooded area above the weir offers a camp site at the end of either track once past the levee bank. Boat launching upstream of the weir is not available. Shore based fishing is available at many locations in the Yanco Creek or in the Murrumbidgee River above the weir.

67. EUROLEY BRIDGE BOAT RAMP

ACCESS ROADS	★★★★
BOAT RAMP	★★★★
CAMPING	NONE
SWIMMING	★
SHORE BASED FISHING	★★
TOILETS	NONE
SHADE	★★★★
BINS	NONE
BARBEQUES	NONE
TABLES/SEATS	NONE

DIRECTIONS

The entrance is 200 m north of Euroley Bridge, 2.4 km from Innisvale Lane, and 5.3 km along Uroly Road from the Irrigation Way intersection.

GPS -34.638583 146.375996

Euroley Bridge boat ramp has 2WD all weather access. Large boats are easily launched off the concrete boat ramp at all water levels. Boats are best launched here if camping nearby (note that camping is not permitted at the boat ramp). Ample car and trailer parking is available. Shore based fishing is limited in space, however there are many kilometres of navigable river providing excellent boat fishing opportunities.

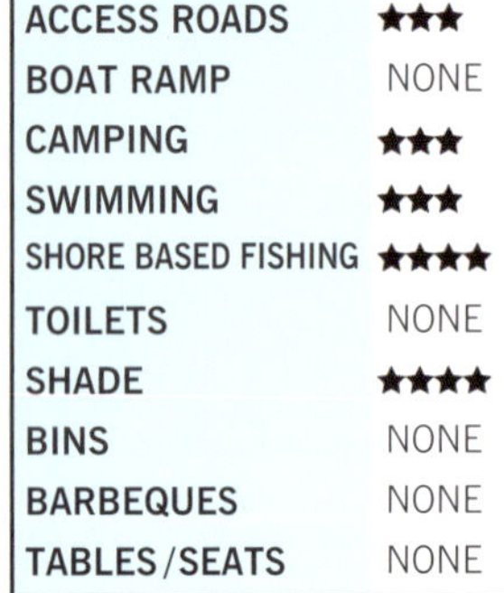

ACCESS ROADS	★★★
BOAT RAMP	NONE
CAMPING	★★★
SWIMMING	★★★
SHORE BASED FISHING	★★★★
TOILETS	NONE
SHADE	★★★★
BINS	NONE
BARBEQUES	NONE
TABLES/SEATS	NONE

68. EUROLEY BRIDGE RESERVE

DIRECTIONS

Turn into Innisvale Lane from the Sturt Highway. Proceed for 6.3 km then turn right at Uroly Road. The main entrance (near the bridge) is 2 km from Innisvale Lane and a secondary entrance is 1.1 km from Innisvale Lane. From Yanco, turn into Uroly Road from Irrigation Way and proceed for 5.8 km to the entrance located immediately south of the bridge.

GPS -34.641424 146.372164

Euroley Bridge is an easily accessible reserve with a sealed road to the entrance. The riverside track eventually loops back onto Uroly Road. This track is not suitable for caravans. Trailer boat launching is best using the concrete boat ramp at Euroley Bridge. Numerous flat, shaded sites are available along the riverside track, which also provides shore based fishing opportunities.

69. MURRUMBIDGEE VALLEY NATIONAL PARK (EUROLEY)

ACCESS ROADS	★★★
BOAT RAMP	★
CAMPING	★★★★
SWIMMING	★★★
SHORE BASED FISHING	★★★★
TOILETS	NONE
SHADE	★★★★★
BINS	NONE
BARBEQUES	NONE
TABLES/SEATS	NONE

DIRECTIONS

Turn into Innisvale Lane from the Sturt Highway. Proceed for 6.3 km, then turn left at Uroly Road. The entrance is 400 m west of the Innisvale Lane and Uroly Road intersection. From Yanco turn into Uroly Road from Irrigation Way and proceed for 8.3 km to the entrance gate.

GPS -34.644046 146.348378

The access tracks through the Murrumbidgee Valley National Park (Euroley) are 4WD and slippery when wet. The track loops through the forest allowing a variety of quality camping and fishing sites to be accessed. Trailer boat launching is limited due to steep banks. However, trailer boats can be launched from the concrete ramp at Euroley Bridge and driven downstream to the chosen campsite.

70. MURRUMBIDGEE VALLEY NATIONAL PARK (MIA 2)

DIRECTIONS

Ski Beach is accessed by turning into Research Road from Irrigation Way at Yanco and following the Ski Beach signs. Middle Beach is accessed from Uroly Road 400 m north of Euroley Bridge (2.6 km from Innisvale Lane) and 5.3 km along Uroly Road from Irrigation Way. Note that the Forest Drive links Middle and Ski Beaches.

GPS -34.637653 146.375966

ACCESS ROADS	★★★
BOAT RAMP	★★★★★
CAMPING	★★★
SWIMMING	★★★★★
SHORE BASED FISHING	★★★
TOILETS	★★★★★
SHADE	★★★★★
BINS	NONE
BARBEQUES	NONE
TABLES/SEATS	NONE

Murrumbidgee Valley National Park (MIA 2) is a large red gum forest with two distinct recreational areas, Ski Beach and Middle Beach. Ski Beach is a popular water skiing park with a concrete ramp, toilets and shaded tables. This area is managed by the Leeton Ski Club and a small fee is charged for use of facilities (an honesty box is near the boat ramp). Middle Beach offers toilet facilities, ample parking and is an ideal swimming and picnic destination. No boat launching is available at Middle Beach, however boats are easily launched at the nearby Euroley Bridge boat ramp. Forest Drive provides access to several other shore based fishing destinations and camping areas that are located at the end of secondary tracks (particularly downstream of Ski Beach).

71. BILLENBAH RESERVE (COLEAMBALLY SKI CLUB)

DIRECTIONS

The entrance is located 3.5 km west of Innisvale Lane along Uroly Road, 10.1 km east of the Banandra property sign along Uroly Road, and 14.1 km east of the Sturt Highway along Uroly Road.

GPS -34.644534 146.317440

ACCESS ROADS	★★★★
BOAT RAMP	★★★
CAMPING	★★★★
SWIMMING	★★★★
SHORE BASED FISHING	★★★
TOILETS	★★★★
SHADE	★★★★
BINS	NONE
BARBEQUES	NONE
TABLES/SEATS	★★★★★

Billenbah is a well-groomed reserve with all-weather access tracks leading to the river and the Coleambally Ski Club facilities. The concrete boat ramp and shaded tables are highlights of this reserve. Boat launching is restricted during low water levels. Billenbah is a popular water skiing location in summer and pride is taken with its appearance and upkeep. Shore based fishing and more secluded camp sites are accessed using a secondary track 200 m before the main camping area.

72. GOGELDRIE WEIR

ACCESS ROADS	★★★★★
BOAT RAMP	★★★★★
CAMPING	★★★★★
SWIMMING	★★★
SHORE BASED FISHING	★★★★★
TOILETS	★★★★★
SHADE	★★★★★
BINS	★★★★★
BARBEQUES	★★★★★
TABLES/SEATS	★★★★★

DIRECTIONS

The entrance is 5.1 km east of Litchfield Road and 100 m west of Gogeldrie Road.

GPS -34.608012 146.255353

Gogeldrie Weir provides a public concrete boat ramp offering all weather launching to the weir pool. A secondary gravel ramp is located on the Sturt Canal, 1.2 km from the Gogeldrie Road entrance, which also provides access to the weir pool. Launching at these ramps is not possible during low water levels. Camping is available along the Sturt Canal, which is suited to caravans. The Canal also offers good shore based fishing opportunities. Access to the Murrumbidgee River below the weir wall is through the Gogeldrie Weir Park for a small charge (shore based fishing below the wall is excellent). The Weir Park also offers paid camping and amenities.

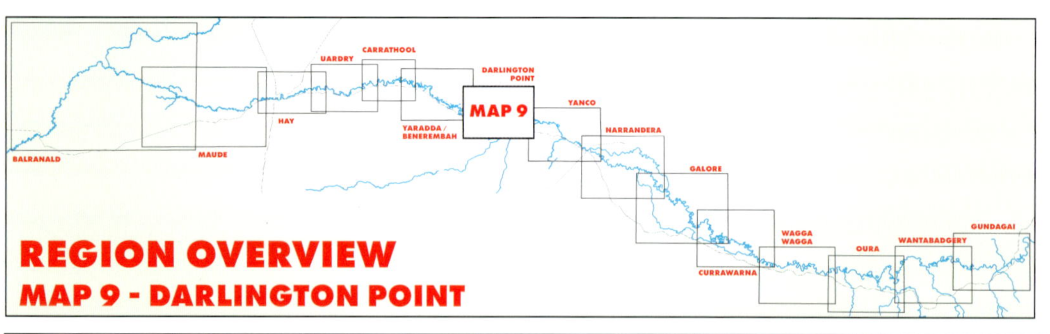

REGION OVERVIEW
MAP 9 - DARLINGTON POINT

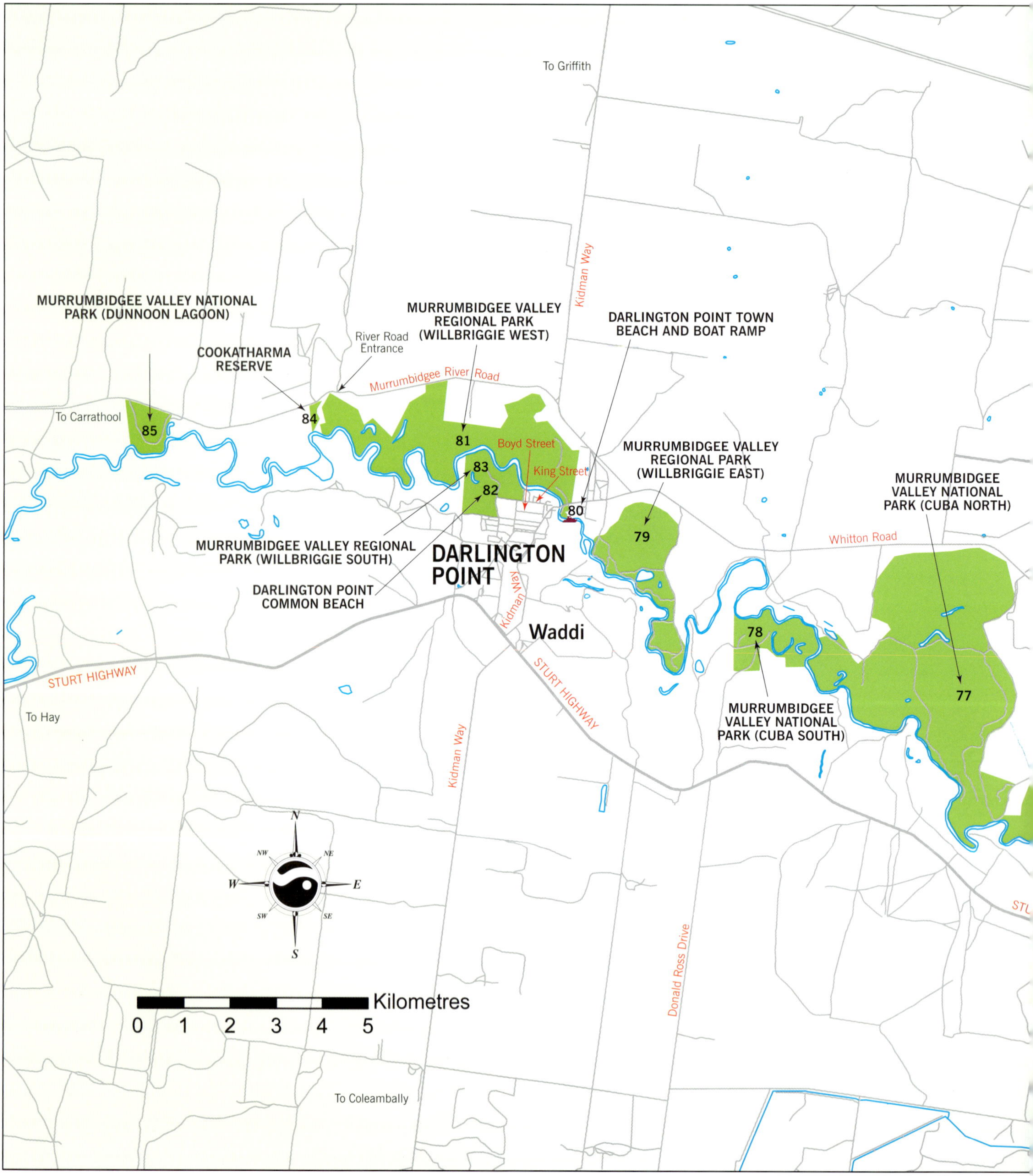

To Griffith

Kidman Way

MURRUMBIDGEE VALLEY NATIONAL PARK (DUNNOON LAGOON)

MURRUMBIDGEE VALLEY REGIONAL PARK (WILLBRIGGIE WEST)

DARLINGTON POINT TOWN BEACH AND BOAT RAMP

COOKATHARMA RESERVE

River Road Entrance

Murrumbidgee River Road

To Carrathool

85

84

81

Boyd Street

83

King Street

82

80

MURRUMBIDGEE VALLEY REGIONAL PARK (WILLBRIGGIE EAST)

79

MURRUMBIDGEE VALLEY NATIONAL PARK (CUBA NORTH)

Whitton Road

MURRUMBIDGEE VALLEY REGIONAL PARK (WILLBRIGGIE SOUTH)

DARLINGTON POINT

DARLINGTON POINT COMMON BEACH

Kidman Way

Waddi

78

STURT HIGHWAY

STURT HIGHWAY

77

To Hay

MURRUMBIDGEE VALLEY NATIONAL PARK (CUBA SOUTH)

Kidman Way

N

NW

NE

W

E

SW

SE

S

Kilometres

0 1 2 3 4 5

Donald Ross Drive

To Coleambally

STU

DARLINGTON POINT REGION

Whitton
Rawle Road
Litchfield Road
Harwood Road
Young Road
Pilkington Road
Demamiel Road
River Road
Forest Road
Dry weather road only
Dry weather road only
No access to Cuba State Forest via Forest Road
75
73
WHITTON PUNT RESERVE
76
74
FIRST GATE RESERVE
Banandra Road
MURRUMBIDGEE VALLEY NATIONAL PARK (MIA 3)
MURRUMBIDGEE VALLEY NATIONAL PARK (JURAMBULA)
Tombullen Storage
Uroly Road
Main Canal Road
To Narrandera
STURT HIGHWAY

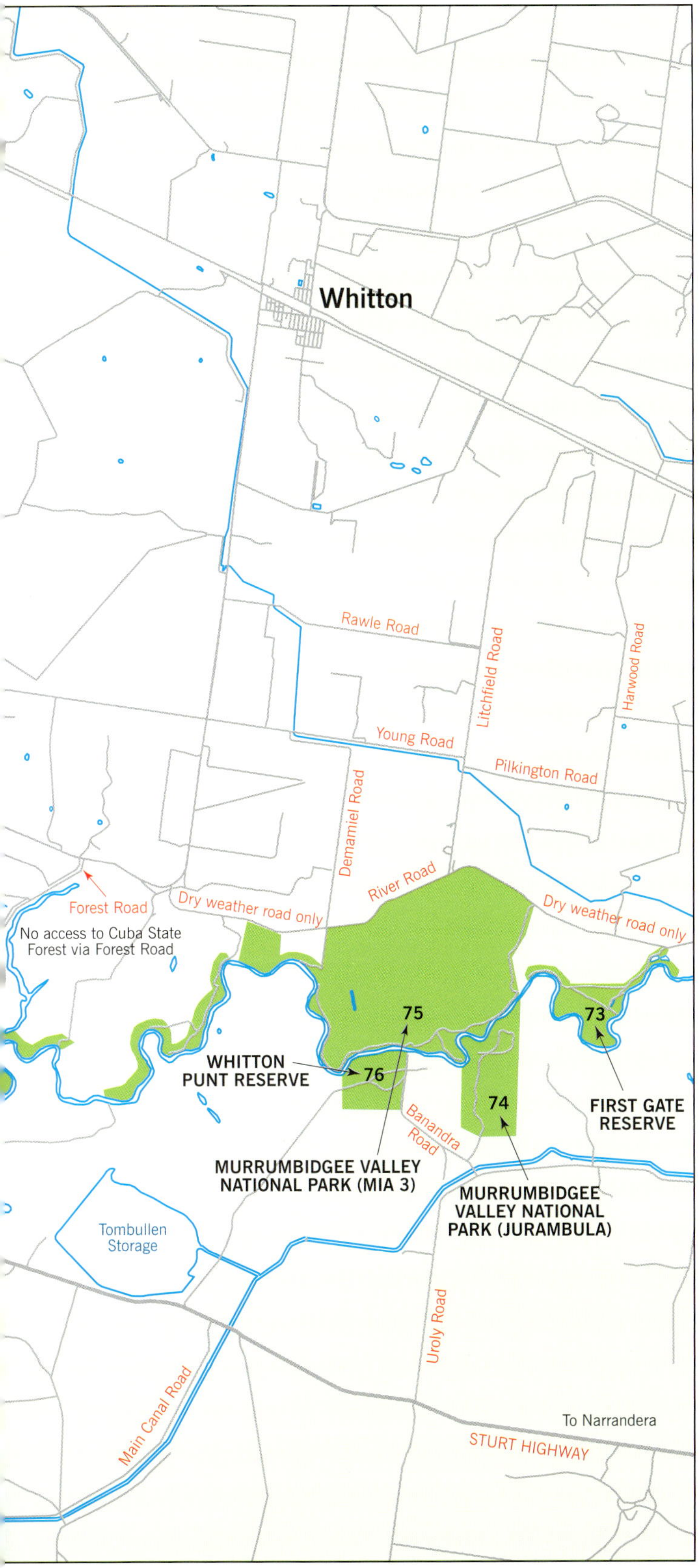

The Darlington Point region is typified by sandy beaches and red gum forest, which make it ideal for camping, picnicking, fishing and swimming. The town of Darlington Point developed around a ford that provided a crossing when the river was low. The crossing was used by bullock teams and stock en route to the Victorian markets or stations on the opposite side of the river. Continued use of the crossing saw the Government reserve land for a future township in the early 1850s. The first property 'Cooba' (named after the Indigenous word 'coob' for a common local tree) was taken up in 1844. River steamers began to work through the region in 1853, with the red gum forests providing fuel for the steamers.

73. FIRST GATE RESERVE

DIRECTIONS

The entrance is 4.2 km west of Litchfield Road and 1.0 km east of Gogeldrie Road.

GPS -34.609329 146.246089

ACCESS ROADS	★★★
BOAT RAMP	★★
CAMPING	★★★★
SWIMMING	★★★★★
SHORE BASED FISHING	★★★
TOILETS	NONE
SHADE	★★★★
BINS	NONE
BARBEQUES	NONE
TABLES/SEATS	NONE

First Gate features numerous open, flat camping areas with sections featuring steep banks or sandy beaches. The beach areas provide excellent swimming and boat launching is possible using 4WD or remote launch. Access tracks are 2WD, but 4WD when wet. Shore based fishing is good on the steeper banks (away from the sandy beaches) where clay drop-offs and snags provide good fish habitat. This reserve is suitable for large groups and can accommodate several camps in isolation from each other.

74. MURRUMBIDGEE VALLEY NATIONAL PARK (JURAMBULA)

ACCESS ROADS	★★★
BOAT RAMP	★
CAMPING	★★★★
SWIMMING	★★★★★
SHORE BASED FISHING	★★★★
TOILETS	NONE
SHADE	★★★★
BINS	NONE
BARBEQUES	NONE
TABLES/SEATS	NONE

DIRECTIONS

The unsealed access road (Banandra Road) leading to Jurambula's entrance is 10.1 km west of Billenbah Reserve, 13.5 km from Innisvale Lane and 4.0 km from the Sturt Highway along Uroly road. Once you turn into Banandra Road, continue over bridge and turn right after 200 m to the entrance.

GPS -34.639420 146.212428

The entrance to Murrumbidgee Valley National Park (Jurambula) is 300 m from the front gate. Jurambula has wide, well-maintained tracks suitable for camping trailers and high clearance caravans. The tracks are 2WD, but 4WD when wet. The main track leads to Maccas Bend (2.1 km from entrance), which offers a sandy beach, excellent swimming and shore based fishing and a large open camp site. Trailer boat launching is a difficult 4WD launch across the beach at Macca's Bend.

75. MURRUMBIDGEE VALLEY NATIONAL PARK (MIA 3)

ACCESS ROADS	★★★★
BOAT RAMP	★★
CAMPING	★★★
SWIMMING	★★★★★
SHORE BASED FISHING	★★★★
TOILETS	NONE
SHADE	★★★★
BINS	NONE
BARBEQUES	NONE
TABLES/SEATS	NONE

DIRECTIONS

The entrance is 1.5 km east of Litchfield Road and 3.5 km west of Gogeldrie Road.

GPS -34.602967 146.223228

Murrumbidgee Valley National Park (MIA 3) is a large area with a long waterfront, but has relatively few accessible camping areas. The available sites are well shaded, flat and open, with excellent swimming. The main track leading from the entrance (Forest Drive) is 2WD (4WD when wet) and continues along the waterfront for approximately 6 km. Camping and boat launching areas (using 4WD or remote launch) are located at 2.4 km and 3.6 km (Whitton Beach) along Forest Drive. This section of river has numerous snags and has excellent shore and boat fishing.

76. WHITTON PUNT RESERVE

ACCESS ROADS	★★★
BOAT RAMP	★★
CAMPING	★★★
SWIMMING	★★★★
SHORE BASED FISHING	★★★
TOILETS	NONE
SHADE	★★★★
BINS	NONE
BARBEQUES	NONE
TABLES/SEATS	NONE

DIRECTIONS

The unsealed access road (Banandra Road) leading to Whitton Punt Reserve is 10.1 km east of Billenbah Reserve, 13.5 km from Innisvale Lane and 4.0 km from the Sturt Highway along Uroly road. Once you turn into Banandra Road, continue over bridge for 2.4 km to the entrance on the left. From the front gates, continue for 400 m to a single gate. Proceed through the date for a further 500 m, then take right track to picnic area and beach (350 m). Note that the main track continues to private property.

GPS -34.626003 146.201219

The Whitton Punt picnic area has good swimming and shaded camping sites. The track continues through the picnic area running parallel to the river giving access to further camping and fishing sites upstream. Trailer boat launching is best at the picnic area using 4WD or remote-launch. Note that areas upstream of the picnic area have limited or no boat launching possibilities, but offer more secluded camping and better shore based fishing.

77. MURRUMBIDGEE VALLEY NATIONAL PARK (CUBA NORTH)

ACCESS ROADS	★★★★
BOAT RAMP	★★★
CAMPING	★★★★
SWIMMING	★★★★
SHORE BASED FISHING	★★★★
TOILETS	NONE
SHADE	★★★★
BINS	NONE
BARBEQUES	NONE
TABLES/SEATS	NONE

DIRECTIONS

The main entrance is located 10.1 km east of the Kidman Way and Whitton Road intersection and 3.5 km west of Forest Road (the entrance is immediately east of the irrigation channel). Proceed 300 m to the National Park entrance grid. Follow the main track (Cuba Drive) along the left hand boundary fence to the main camping areas.

GPS -34.582698 146.111270

Murrumbidgee Valley National Park (Cuba North) is an extremely large area offering good access to the river and numerous campsites via good quality tracks. River Drive follows the river and provides access to sandy beaches and cliff camp sites. Cuba North is a popular camping destination with large, open, well-shaded camps. Shore based fishing and boating is excellent with ideal fish habitat. Boats may be launched from beach areas (e.g. Cuba Beach) using 4WD or remote-launch.

78. MURRUMBIDGEE VALLEY NATIONAL PARK (CUBA SOUTH)

DIRECTIONS

The entrance is 150 m east of Donald Ross Drive and 13.0 km west of Main Canal Road.

GPS -34.620102 146.038713

ACCESS ROADS	★★★
BOAT RAMP	★
CAMPING	★★★★
SWIMMING	★★★
SHORE BASED FISHING	★★★★
TOILETS	NONE
SHADE	★★★★
BINS	NONE
BARBEQUES	NONE
TABLES/SEATS	NONE

Murrumbidgee Valley National Park (Cuba South) is accessed by continuing through the front gate (i.e. between the fences) for 2.2 km. Once in the National Park take the main track (right) as it follow the eastern boundary fence. The river can be accessed by turning left after 1 km (signposted 'river access'), which leads to several open, flat camp sites, a beach and boat launching area. Continuing along the boundary fence track for 700 m leads to a large open campsite on top a high bank. Note that the boundary fence track has boggy, low-lying areas, small creeks and is slippery when wet. 4WD is recommended throughout the National Park with difficult access for caravans. Boat launching is possible by 4WD remote launch across the beach (located at the end of the signposted 'river access' track). Swimming is best at the beach and there are many excellent shore based fishing locations throughout the Park.

79. MURRUMBIDGEE VALLEY REGIONAL PARK (WILLBRIGGIE EAST)

ACCESS ROADS	★★★
BOAT RAMP	★★★
CAMPING	★★★★
SWIMMING	★★★★★
SHORE BASED FISHING	★★★★
TOILETS	NONE
SHADE	★★★★
BINS	NONE
BARBEQUES	NONE
TABLES/SEATS	NONE

DIRECTIONS

The access road leading to the front gate is 300 m east of the Kidman Way and Whitton Road intersection. The Park entrance is 400 m along this unsealed road. A second entrance is accessed from Whitton Road, 2.2 km from the main entrance (-34.570207 146.031923). This unnamed entrance leads to Black Box Road.

GPS -34.567745 146.013651

Murrumbidgee Valley Regional Park (Willbriggie East) is a large area with two entrances accessing approximately 7 km of riverfront. Featured in this Park are several beach camps capable of accommodating large groups. These campsites are signposted and ideal for family groups with excellent swimming at shallow, sandy beaches. Between the beach areas, river bends offer ample fish habitat and excellent angling. Tracks are 2WD when dry and 4WD when wet. Boat launching is available with 4WD or remote-launch across the various beaches.

80. DARLINGTON POINT TOWN BEACH AND BOAT RAMP

ACCESS ROADS	★★★★
BOAT RAMP	★★★★★
CAMPING	NONE
SWIMMING	★★★★
SHORE BASED FISHING	★★★
TOILETS	NONE
SHADE	★★★
BINS	★★★★★
BARBEQUES	NONE
TABLES/SEATS	★★★★★

DIRECTIONS

The entrance road is between the bridges on the northern bank of the river. The road to the boat ramp and beach is signposted and accessed by turning right immediately before the caravan park entrance.

GPS -34.568650 146.005245

Darlington Point Town Beach has an excellent concrete boat ramp allowing launching of all sized watercraft. The adjacent picnic area has shaded tables and manicured grass providing an ideal location for a family picnic or rest stop for travellers. No camping is permitted at Town Beach; it is designed for day visitors only. There is ample parking at the ramp for boats, caravans and cars. Swimming at the beach area is good however strong currents can be hazardous.

81. MURRUMBIDGEE VALLEY REGIONAL PARK (WILLBRIGGIE WEST)

DIRECTIONS

The entrance is 27.2 km east of Griffith Bringagee Road and 5.4 km west of the Murrumbidgee River Road and Kidman Way intersection. The town entrance is accessed by turning north from the Kidman Way between the two bridges.

GPS -34.548402 145.947344

ACCESS ROADS	★★★★
BOAT RAMP	★★
CAMPING	★★★★
SWIMMING	★★★★
SHORE BASED FISHING	★★★★
TOILETS	NONE
SHADE	★★★★
BINS	NONE
BARBEQUES	NONE
TABLES/SEATS	NONE

Murrumbidgee Valley Regional Park (Willbriggie West) is a large area with two entrances linked by approximately 10 km of scenic forest drive that generally parallels the waterfront. Willbriggie West has numerous camping, fishing and boat launching locations and is featured by a beach and large open, flat campsite, 1.5 km from the River Road entrance. This Park is popular during the warmer months with more secluded campsites located at the ends of secondary trails stemming from the main track. The River Road entrance is a shorter distance from the road to the main beach, than the town entrance.

ACCESS ROADS	★★★★
BOAT RAMP	★★
CAMPING	★★★★
SWIMMING	★★★
SHORE BASED FISHING	★★★★
TOILETS	NONE
SHADE	★★★★
BINS	★★★
BARBEQUES	NONE
TABLES/SEATS	★★

82. DARLINGTON POINT COMMON BEACH

DIRECTIONS

From the Sturt Highway turn north into Kidman Way. From the Kidman Way, turn into Boyd Street and then immediately right into Carrington Lane. At the end of Carrington Lane, turn left into King Street and proceed over the levee to reserve entrance.

GPS -34.567733 145.992772

Darlington Point Common Beach has a loop track leading to camp sites and shore based fishing locations. The tracks are 2WD, but 4WD in wet weather. Boat launching is available for 4WD or remote launch across the beach. River access is limited due to steep banks, however steep clay drop-offs offer excellent angling opportunities. Swimming is good at the beach area, whilst flat, well-shaded sites are ideal for camping.

83. MURRUMBIDGEE VALLEY REGIONAL PARK (WILLBRIGGIE SOUTH)

ACCESS ROADS	★★★★
BOAT RAMP	★★
CAMPING	★★★
SWIMMING	★★
SHORE BASED FISHING	★★★★
TOILETS	NONE
SHADE	★★★★
BINS	NONE
BARBEQUES	NONE
TABLES/SEATS	NONE

DIRECTIONS

From the Sturt Highway turn north into Kidman Way. From the Kidman Way, turn into Boyd Street and then immediately right into Carrington Lane. At the end of Carrington Lane, turn left into King Street and proceed over the levee into Darlington Point Common Beach. Follow the left hand track for 300 m, then turn right and continue for a further 300 m. Veer left, then continue straight for 200 m to the entrance grid.

GPS -34.563628 145.987968

Murrumbidgee Valley Regional Park (Willbriggie South) offers a kilometre of secluded camping and shore based fishing locations. These sites are accessed from the main road using the secondary tracks. The tracks are 2WD, but 4WD in wet weather. Boat launching is available for 4WD or remote launch at a site 500 m from the entrance grid.

84. COOKATHARMA RESERVE

DIRECTIONS

The entrance is 27.1 km east of Griffith Bringagee Road and 5.5 km west of the Murrumbidgee River Road and Kidman Way intersection (note that the entrance is located adjacent to the Murrumbidgee Valley National Park (Willbriggie West entrance).

ACCESS ROADS	★★★
BOAT RAMP	★★★
CAMPING	★★★★
SWIMMING	★★★
SHORE BASED FISHING	★★★
TOILETS	NONE
SHADE	★★★★
BINS	NONE
BARBEQUES	NONE
TABLES/SEATS	NONE

GPS -34.548482 145.947562

Cookatharma has a single, open campsite with limited river frontage. This camp could accommodate a large group and has good shade and easy trailer boat launching (4WD or remote-launch). The access tracks are 2WD, but 4WD when wet. This area is suitable for caravans and camping trailers. Shore based fishing is good with ample access to the waterfront.

85. MURRUMBIDGEE VALLEY NATIONAL PARK (DUNNOON LAGOON)

ACCESS ROADS	★★★★
BOAT RAMP	★★
CAMPING	★★★★
SWIMMING	★★★★
SHORE BASED FISHING	★★★★
TOILETS	NONE
SHADE	★★★★★
BINS	NONE
BARBEQUES	NONE
TABLES/SEATS	NONE

DIRECTIONS

The entrance is 22.7 km east of Griffith Bringagee Road and 9.9 km west of the Murrumbidgee River Road and Kidman Way intersection.

GPS -34.548591 145.901708

Access roads into Murrumbidgee Valley National Park (Dunnoon Lagoon) are 2WD (4WD when wet). Nobles Beach (left hand track) and Platypus Beach (right hand track) are signposted and offer large, open flat campsites under shaded gums. These beaches allow boat launching using 4WD or remote launch. The track quality and campsite size allow access for caravans and camping trailers at Nobles Beach. The track to Platypus Beach is not suited to caravans. The main track follows the riverfront downstream giving access to more secluded camping and fishing locations.

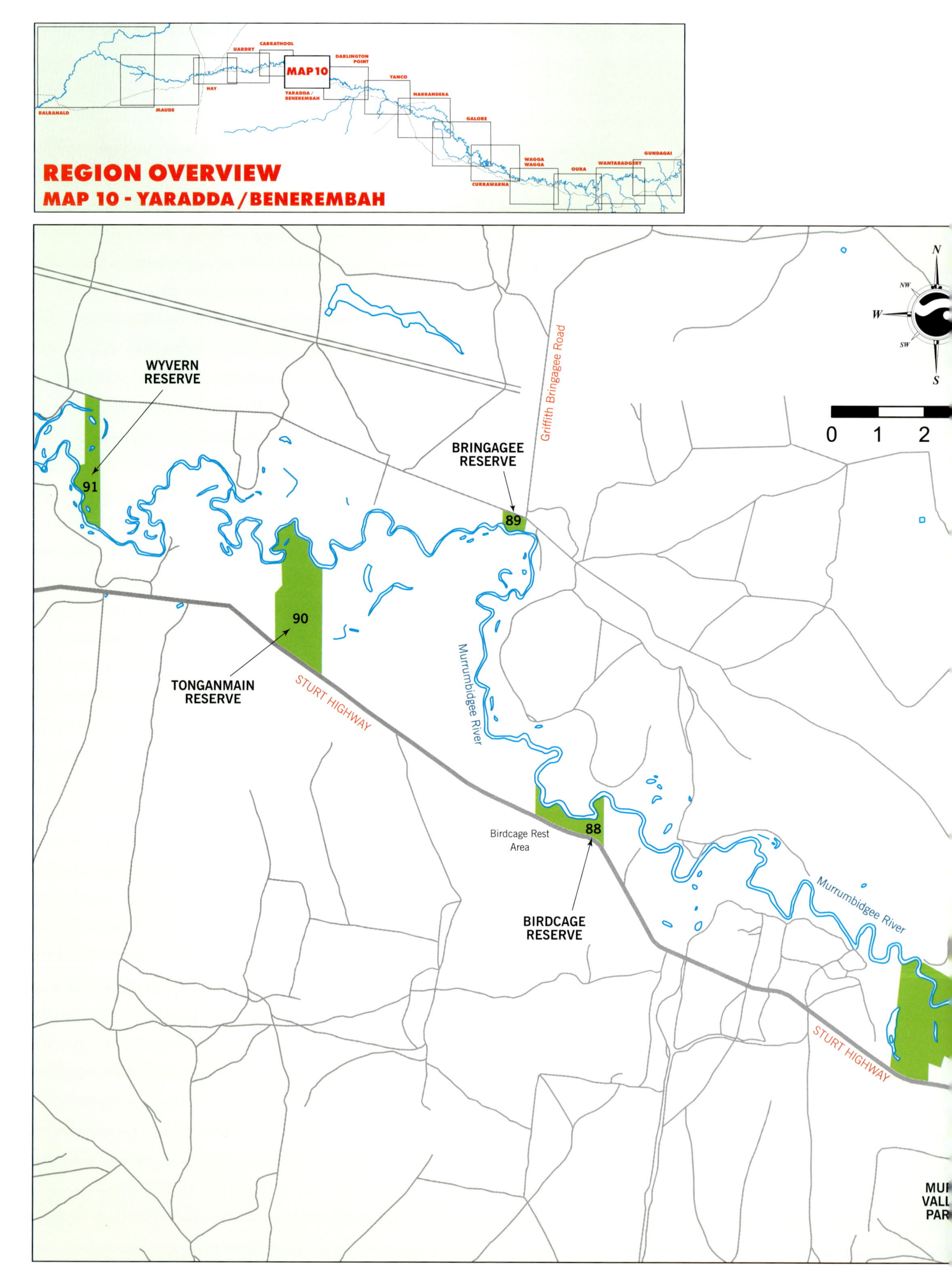

REGION OVERVIEW
MAP 10 - YARADDA / BENEREMBAH
BALRANALD
MAUDE
HAY
UARDRY
CARRATHOOL
MAP 10
DARLINGTON POINT
YARADDA / BENEREMBAH
YANCO
NARRANDERA
GALORE
WAGGA WAGGA
CURRAWARNA
OURA
WANTABADGERY
GUNDAGAI
WYVERN RESERVE
91
BRINGAGEE RESERVE
89
Griffith Bringagee Road
90
TONGANMAIN RESERVE
STURT HIGHWAY
Murrumbidgee River
88
Birdcage Rest Area
BIRDCAGE RESERVE
Murrumbidgee River
STURT HIGHWAY
N
NW
W
SW
S
0 1 2

YARADDA/BENEREMBAH REGION

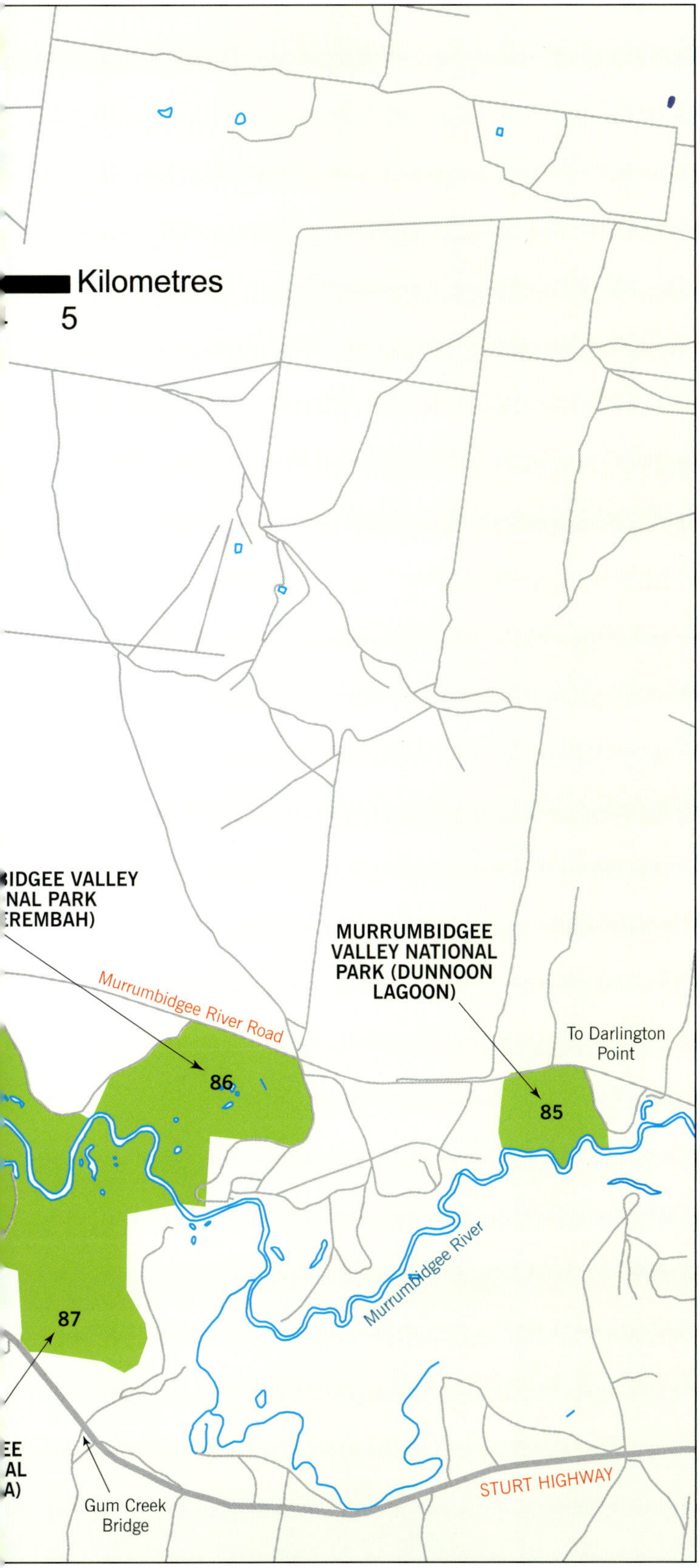

Kilometres
5

IDGEE VALLEY
NAL PARK
EREMBAH)

MURRUMBIDGEE
VALLEY NATIONAL
PARK (DUNNOON
LAGOON)

Murrumbidgee River Road

To Darlington
Point

86

85

Murrumbidgee River

87

EE
AL
A)

Gum Creek
Bridge

STURT HIGHWAY

The red gum forests and wetlands in this region have national and international status in recognition of their natural and cultural values. Lined by iconic river red gums, the rivers and wetlands are popular for a variety of recreational activities including bushwalking, bird watching, picnicking, four-wheel driving, fishing and boating. Periodic river flooding provides the water needed for growth and regeneration of the forests in what is basically an arid landscape. Cockatoos, parrots, robins and kingfishers are just a few of the species of birds that can be seen in these forests. The area is popular with birdwatchers from around the world, who visit the forest, lakes and lagoons to see waterbirds including pelicans, swans, cormorants, ibis, spoonbills and many types of duck.

86. MURRUMBIDGEE VALLEY NATIONAL PARK (BENEREMBAH)

DIRECTIONS

The entrance is 16.7 km east of Griffith Bringagee Road (eastern side of the levee bank) and 15.7 km west of the Murrumbidgee River Road and Kidman Way intersection.

GPS -34.542776 145.840291

ACCESS ROADS	★★★
BOAT RAMP	★★★
CAMPING	★★★★
SWIMMING	★★★
SHORE BASED FISHING	★★★★
TOILETS	NONE
SHADE	★★★★
BINS	NONE
BARBEQUES	NONE
TABLES/SEATS	NONE

Benerembah is a large area that is divided into eastern and western sections by an irrigation canal. The eastern section is accessed by following the signs to Daryls Beach and Bream Bend. These areas provide open, flat campsites. Boat launching is available by 4WD or remote launch across Daryls Beach. The western section of Benerembah is accessed by turning right from the main track over the grid, 1.7 km from the main entrance. Cross over the canal and follow River Road to access numerous excellent camping areas. The western section offers the best boat launch, which is also located off River Road at -34.558151 145.820889. Access to most of the waterfront is restricted by steep banks, however these areas provides excellent shore based fishing opportunities. Tracks are impassable in wet weather.

87. MURRUMBIDGEE VALLEY NATIONAL PARK (YARADDA)

DIRECTIONS

The entrance is 4.4 km west of Gum Creek Bridge and 9.8 km east of the Birdcage Rest Area.

GPS -34.574912 145.784506

ACCESS ROADS	★★★
BOAT RAMP	★★★
CAMPING	★★★★
SWIMMING	★★
SHORE BASED FISHING	★★★★
TOILETS	NONE
SHADE	★★★★
BINS	NONE
BARBEQUES	NONE
TABLES/SEATS	NONE

Murrumbidgee Valley National Park (Yaradda) is a large area with reasonable quality roads that access over 15 km of waterfront. The track from the gate to the river (Forest Drive) is 2.0 km long and where this road meets the river there are several large, open areas for camping on top of the high bank. The track heading downstream leads to Norm's Beach, which has a gently sloping bank where trailer boats may be launched. This camp also has good shade, flat ground and easy access to the water for shore based fishing. The track leading upstream is approximately 10 km long providing numerous opportunities for secluded camps and excellent shore based fishing. Note that the bank upstream is generally steep which reduces boat launching and swimming opportunities.

88. BIRDCAGE RESERVE

ACCESS ROADS	★★★
BOAT RAMP	★★★
CAMPING	★★★★
SWIMMING	★★
SHORE BASED FISHING	★★★★
TOILETS	★★★★★
SHADE	★★★★
BINS	★★★★★
BARBEQUES	NONE
TABLES/SEATS	★★★★★

DIRECTIONS

The entrance track is 13.3 km west of Gum Creek Bridge and is on the apex of the Sturt Highway road bend, approximately 1 km east of the Birdcage Rest Area. The western end of the reserve can be accessed from the Birdcage Rest Area using the track behind the toilet block. A second entrance is located 700 m west of the toilet block.

GPS -34.526023 145.702753

Birdcage Reserve has many tracks leading to open, flat areas suitable for caravans. Tracks are 2WD when dry and 4WD when wet. Trailer boat launching is available at the eastern edge of the reserve using the dirt ramp (-34.524938 145.711334). Shore based fishing is excellent with deep snaggy water along the riverfront. The river can also be accessed on the western side of the rest area using the dirt track. This area also has a dirt ramp for boat launching using 4WD or remote launch. The western end of Birdcage has large, open areas on top of high banks. Swimming is poor due to deep water and steep banks.

89. BRINGAGEE RESERVE

DIRECTIONS

The entrance is 27.1 km east of Carrathool Road and 300 m west of Griffith Bringagee Road.

GPS -34.466959 145.693333

ACCESS ROADS	★★★★
BOAT RAMP	★★★★
CAMPING	★★★★
SWIMMING	★★★★
SHORE BASED FISHING	★★★
TOILETS	NONE
SHADE	★★★★★
BINS	NONE
BARBEQUES	NONE
TABLES/SEATS	NONE

Bringagee is a small reserve with a single main campsite and limited river frontage. The campsite is open and flat with good river access for fishing, swimming and boat launching (4WD or remote launch). Large mature trees provide excellent shade and the tracks are 2WD accessible, but 4WD when wet. This reserve is suited to large groups and caravans.

90. TONGANMAIN RESERVE

ACCESS ROADS	★★★
BOAT RAMP	★★★
CAMPING	★★★★
SWIMMING	★★★
SHORE BASED FISHING	★★★★
TOILETS	NONE
SHADE	★★★★
BINS	NONE
BARBEQUES	NONE
TABLES/SEATS	NONE

DIRECTIONS

The entrance is 6.5 km west of the Birdcage Rest Area and 20.4 km east of Conargo Road.

GPS -34.495212 145.644428

Tonganmain offers excellent camping areas. The main track is 2WD, but 4WD when wet. The best campsites are located 2.6 km and 3.0 km from the front gate (veer left at 2.0 km). The first has open, flat areas on a high bank, but no boat launching. The second is a small beach camp. Boat launching using 4WD or remote launch is available over the beach area. Swimming and shore based fishing at the beach camp are good. There is a further campsite at the eastern boundary of the reserve (take right hand track, 2.0 km from entrance) that offers good shore based fishing opportunities, but has no boat launching.

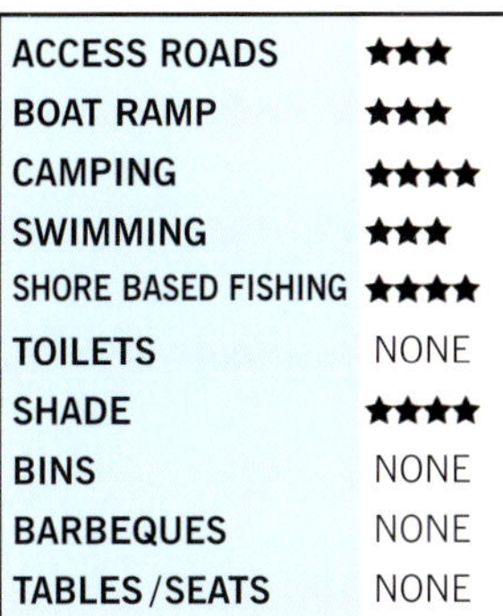

91. WYVERN RESERVE

DIRECTIONS

The entrance is 17.3 km east of the Carrathool Road and Murrumbidgee River Road intersection and 9.7 km west of the Griffith Bringagee Road.

GPS -34.443843 145.594309

ACCESS ROADS	★★★
BOAT RAMP	NONE
CAMPING	★★★
SWIMMING	★
SHORE BASED FISHING	★★★★
TOILETS	NONE
SHADE	★★★★
BINS	NONE
BARBEQUES	NONE
TABLES/SEATS	NONE

Wyvern is a heavily timbered reserve with a network of tracks. The main track forks at 1.6 km from the entrance. The right fork leads to the main camping area, which has flat, open sites on top of a steep bank, but does not allow boat launching. The left fork winds through forested areas eventually leading to several camp sites. These are suitable for shore based fishing and do not allow boat launching. Shore based fishing opportunities are good by walking the bank targeting the ample snags along the steep banks.

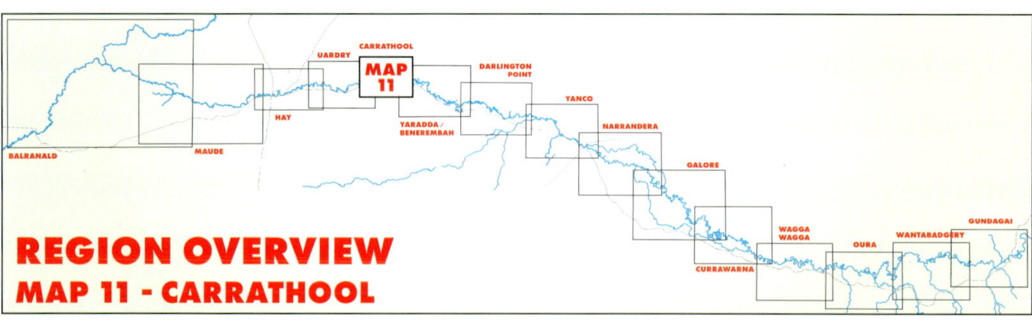

N
NW
NE
W
E
SW
SE
S

Kilometres
0
1.5
3

CARRATHOOL

Wrights Lane

OLD CURRATHOOL RESERVE (DEAD FINISH)

PINKER'S BEACH

Murrumbidgee River Road

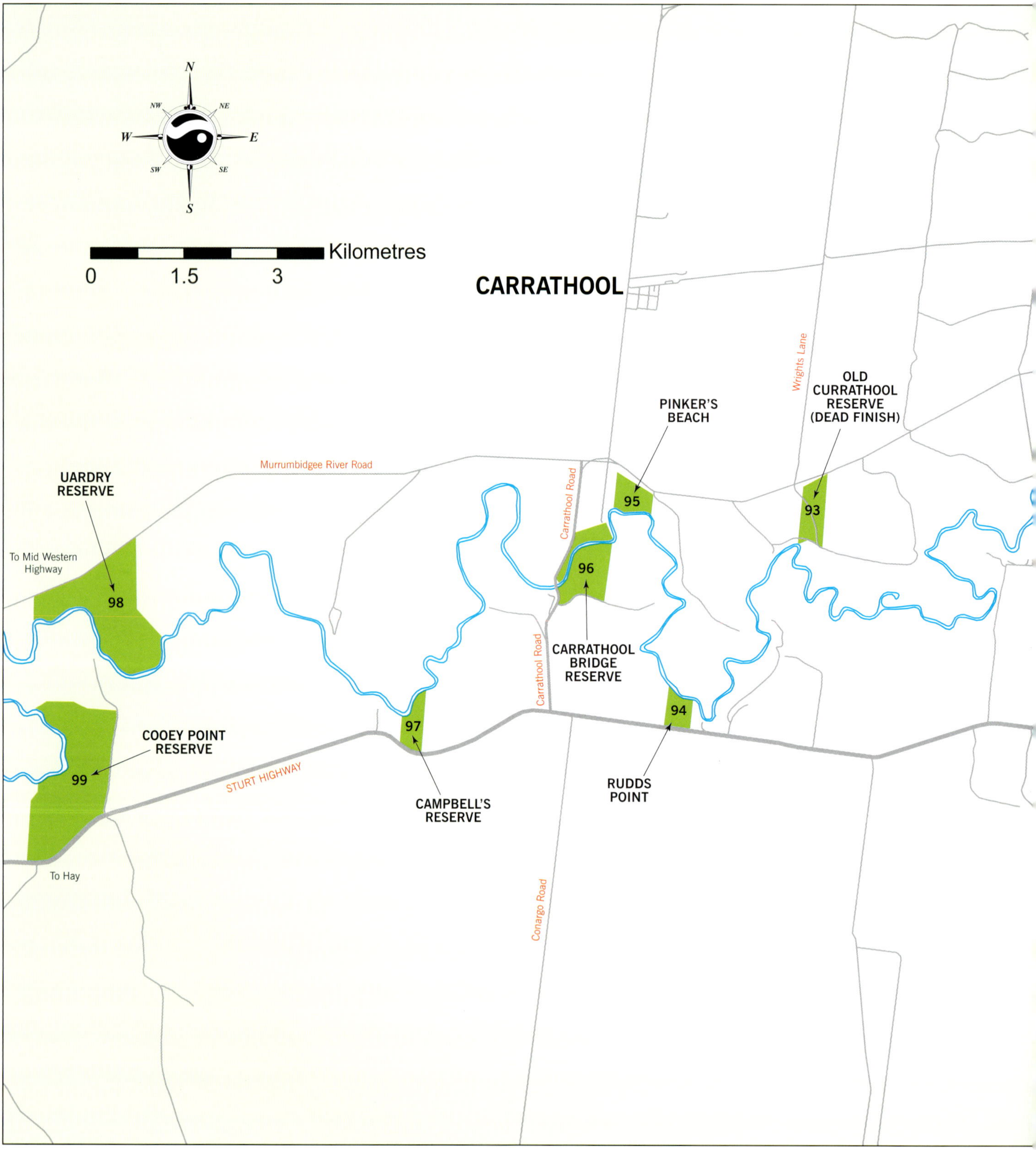

Carrathool Road

UARDRY RESERVE

95

93

To Mid Western Highway

96

98

CARRATHOOL BRIDGE RESERVE

Carrathool Road

94

97

COOEY POINT RESERVE

99

STURT HIGHWAY

RUDDS POINT

CAMPBELL'S RESERVE

To Hay

Conargo Road

CARRATHOOL REGION

Charles Sturt was probably the first European to pass through the Carrathool region during his exploration of the inland river system in 1829. Carrathool began its life as a way station serving travellers between Narrandera and Hay. The railway arrived on the northern side of the river in 1882, which is the site of the present township. With both trains and river steamers, Carrathool became a bustling port and rail-head serving Hillston, Cobar, the copper mine at Mt Hope and the sheep, timber, wool, cattle and wheat producers of the surrounding area. The depression of the 1930s, removal of the shire headquarters to Goolgowi in 1934 and the development of the highway system in the post-war years eroded Carrathool's importance as a service centre and it exists today as a small rural community.

WEBB'S RESERVE
92
Murrumbidgee River Road
To Darlington Point
91
WYVERN RESERVE
STURT HIGHWAY

92. WEBB'S RESERVE

ACCESS ROADS	★★★
BOAT RAMP	★★★
CAMPING	★★★★
SWIMMING	★★★
SHORE BASED FISHING	★★★★
TOILETS	NONE
SHADE	★★★★
BINS	NONE
BARBEQUES	NONE
TABLES/SEATS	NONE

DIRECTIONS

The entrance is located opposite cattle yards, 9.6 km east of the Carrathool Road and Murrumbidgee River Road intersection and 17.3 km west of the Griffith Bringagee Road.

GPS -34.421946 145.518033

Webb's Reserve features two main campsites located at the eastern and western boundaries. The campsites are linked by a rough track which runs alongside the river. Both camps offer flat, open shaded camping with good shore based fishing. Trailer boat launching (4WD or remote-launch) is better at the western campsite. The tracks are reasonable, but 4WD when wet.

93. OLD CURRATHOOL RESERVE (DEAD FINISH)

DIRECTIONS

The access road is 3.5 km east of the Carrathool Road and Murrumbidgee River Road intersection (on the eastern side of the irrigation channel) and 23.8 km west of the Griffith Bringagee Road.

GPS -34.437024 145.459496

Old Currathool offers 50 m of river frontage in the south west corner (beside the house). This area has good shade and swimming and the gently sloping bank allows for trailer boat launching. Tracks to the river are 2WD, but are slippery when wet. Shore based fishing is good, but the short length of waterfront can restrict angling options.

ACCESS ROADS	★★★★
BOAT RAMP	★★★★
CAMPING	★★★
SWIMMING	★★★
SHORE BASED FISHING	★★★
TOILETS	NONE
SHADE	★★★
BINS	NONE
BARBEQUES	NONE
TABLES/SEATS	NONE

94. RUDD'S POINT

DIRECTIONS

The entrance is 26.5 km west of the Birdcage Rest Area and 1.7 km east of Conargo Road.

GPS -34.471093 145.439838

Rudd's Point is a small reserve with limited river frontage. It has excellent trailer boat launching at the western boundary camp, but better fishing at the upstream boundary. Camping is good with large trees and open areas. Several large groups can be accommodated despite it not being a large physical area. The access tracks are 2WD, but are slippery when wet.

ACCESS ROADS	★★★★
BOAT RAMP	★★★★
CAMPING	★★★
SWIMMING	★★★
SHORE BASED FISHING	★★★
TOILETS	NONE
SHADE	★★★★
BINS	NONE
BARBEQUES	NONE
TABLES/SEATS	NONE

95. PINKER'S BEACH

DIRECTIONS

The entrance is 500 m east of the Carrathool Road and Murrumbidgee River Road intersection and 26.9 km west of the Griffith Bringagee Road.

GPS -34.433966 145.428345

ACCESS ROADS	★★★★
BOAT RAMP	★★★
CAMPING	★★★★
SWIMMING	★★★★
SHORE BASED FISHING	★★★
TOILETS	★★★★
SHADE	★★★★
BINS	NONE
BARBEQUES	NONE
TABLES/SEATS	NONE

Pinker's Beach offers open expanses, large shady trees and gently sloping access to the river, which makes it an ideal camping, swimming and boating location. Large groups are catered for with space for many camps. Pinker's has a toilet block and is suitable for caravans. Shore based fishing is best above and below the shallow beach area. Trailer boat launching is best at the main camping area using 4WD or remote-launch. Numerous mid-river snags provide excellent boat fishing.

96. CARRATHOOL BRIDGE RESERVE

DIRECTIONS

The entrance is 1.8 km along Carrathool Road from the Sturt Highway. To access the southern side, turn east just before the bridge and then left over the culvert to the river. To access the northern shore turn east from Carrathool Road immediately once over the bridge (or before bridge if approaching from Carrathool).

GPS -34.447932 145.418687

ACCESS ROADS	★★★★
BOAT RAMP	NONE
CAMPING	★★★
SWIMMING	★★
SHORE BASED FISHING	★★★
TOILETS	NONE
SHADE	★★★
BINS	NONE
BARBEQUES	NONE
TABLES/SEATS	★★★★★

Carrathool Bridge Reserve has camping areas on both sides of the river. The southern shore offers more secluded campsites on top of a high bank. The northern shore offers shaded tables and seats and open, flat sites. Trailer boat launching options are not available at southern or northern areas. Shore based fishing is good on both sides with 2WD access tracks (4WD when wet). This area is ideal for shore based fishing and is suitable for caravans.

97. CAMPBELL'S RESERVE

ACCESS ROADS	★★★
BOAT RAMP	★★★
CAMPING	★★★★
SWIMMING	★★★
SHORE BASED FISHING	★★★★
TOILETS	NONE
SHADE	★★★★
BINS	NONE
BARBEQUES	NONE
TABLES/SEATS	NONE

DIRECTIONS

The entrance is on the western side of the irrigation canal, 2.4 km west of the Carrathool Road and 35.8 km east of Glencoe Road.

GPS -34.474007 145.392482

Campbell's has a large camping area on the western side of the irrigation canal with shaded, flat sites on top of a high bank. This area is suitable for caravans, has good shore based fishing, but no boat launching. However, if you cross the levee and turn left there is an excellent campsite with easy trailer boat launching (4WD or remote-launch). This site (adjacent to the pumps) is well shaded and suitable for large camps. The track following the eastern boundary leads to more secluded camping but has difficult 4WD boat launching. These tracks are 2WD, but slippery when wet. Shore based fishing is good.

UARDRY
CARRATHOOL
MAP 12
DARLINGTON POINT
HAY
YANCO
YARADDA / BENEREMBAH
NARRANDERA
BALRANALD
MAUDE
GALORE
GUNDAGAI
WAGGA WAGGA
WANTABADGERY
OURA
CURRAWARNA

REGION OVERVIEW
MAP 12 - UARDRY

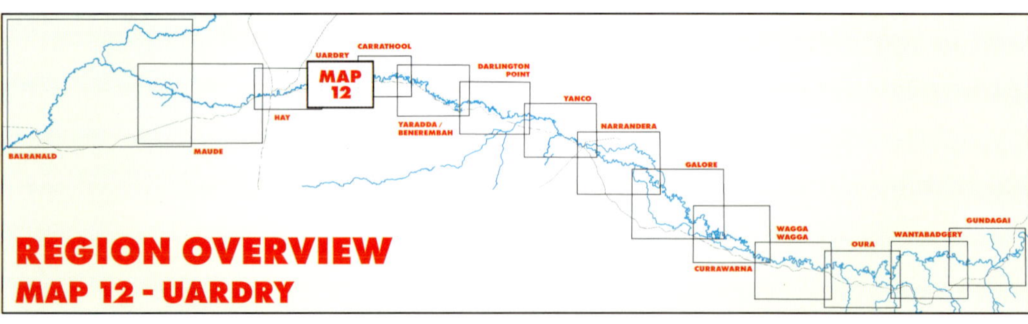

NULABOR RESERVE
To Hay via Mid Western Highway
Murrumbidgee River Road
103
TOM'S POINT RESERVE
100
To Hay
STURT HIGHWAY
102
101
BURRABOGIE RESERVE
MULBERRYGONG RESERVE

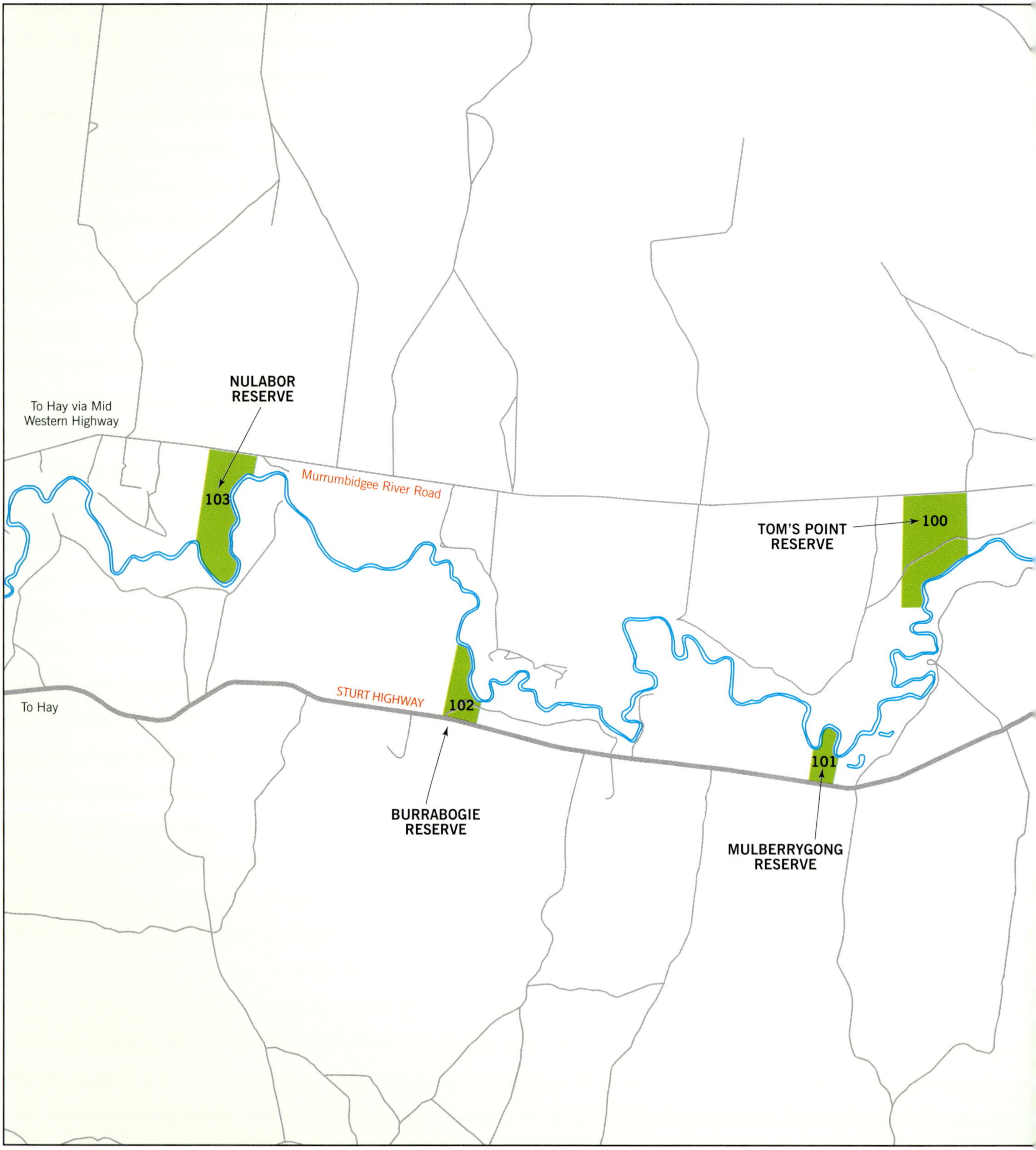

UARDRY REGION

The Uardry region is typified by flat plains and large properties on both sides of the river. This region grew in the 1850s when cattle breeders reaped the benefits of the gold rush by selling stock to hungry miners on the New South Wales and Victorian goldfields. Uardry became famous for its merino sheep that were introduced in 1864. Subsequently, Uardry became a significant merino stud producing a distinct strain—big-framed, with bold fronts and premium quality wool. The sheep were so distinctive that one of the rams was used on the Australian shilling coin. The harsh climate has been circumvented to a degree in recent times by significant irrigation works. Uardry is translated from the local Indigenous dialect as yellow-box tree.

To Carrathool
UARDRY RESERVE
98
Murrumbidgee River Road
99
97
COOEY POINT RESERVE
CAMPBELL'S RESERVE
HIGHWAY
N
NW
NE
W
E
SW
SE
S
Kilometres
0 0.5 1 2 3 4 5

98. UARDRY RESERVE

ACCESS ROADS	★★★★
BOAT RAMP	★★★
CAMPING	★★★★
SWIMMING	★★★★
SHORE BASED FISHING	★★★
TOILETS	NONE
SHADE	★★★★
BINS	NONE
BARBEQUES	NONE
TABLES / SEATS	NONE

DIRECTIONS

The access track is 33.4 km east of the Mid-Western Highway and 9.4 km west of Carrathool Road.

GPS -34.451852 145.324851

Uardry is a large reserve characterised by tall, steep banks. The best camping is at the end of the main access track. This camp extends along a gently sloping bank, with good shade and 4WD trailer boat launching. The secondary track to the left (before you descend to the river from the main track) follows the river upstream leading to additional campsites and shore based fishing locations. Access tracks are 2WD, but slippery when wet. Shore based fishing is good with deep water on the bends and large snags providing excellent fish habitat. Swimming is best at the boat launch site.

99. COOEY POINT RESERVE

DIRECTIONS

The entrance is 9.4 km west of Carrathool Road and 29.0 km east of Glencoe Road.

GPS -34.488568 145.324200

ACCESS ROADS	★★★
BOAT RAMP	★★★
CAMPING	★★★★
SWIMMING	★★
SHORE BASED FISHING	★★★
TOILETS	NONE
SHADE	★★★★
BINS	NONE
BARBEQUES	NONE
TABLES / SEATS	NONE

Cooey Point is a large reserve with two main camp areas. These are accessed by continuing 1.2 km along the track from the gate. Both sites offer flat, open camping on top of a high bank. Boat launching is available using 4WD or remote launch at the downstream camp. The tracks are in good condition but are 4WD only in wet weather. There are numerous shore based fishing opportunities.

100. TOM'S POINT RESERVE

ACCESS ROADS	★★★
BOAT RAMP	★★
CAMPING	★★★
SWIMMING	★★
SHORE BASED FISHING	★★★★
TOILETS	NONE
SHADE	★★★★
BINS	NONE
BARBEQUES	NONE
TABLES/SEATS	NONE

DIRECTIONS

The entrance is 26.5 km east of the Mid-Western Highway along the Murrumbidgee River Road and 16.7 km west of Carrathool Road.

GPS -34.468179 145.256111

Tom's Point main camping area is accessed from the single access track leading into the reserve. This campsite is an open, flat area with good shade and a bank that provides 4WD remote launching. Shore based fishing is good with plenty of sunken timber. The second campsite is found at the upstream boundary of the reserve by following the main track and then turning left before you descend down the bank. Follow the track adjacent to the boundary fence to access the campsite. This camp is only suitable for shore based fishing as no boat launching is possible.

101. MULBERRYGONG RESERVE

ACCESS ROADS	★★★
BOAT RAMP	★★★
CAMPING	★★★★
SWIMMING	★★
SHORE BASED FISHING	★★★★
TOILETS	NONE
SHADE	★★★★
BINS	NONE
BARBEQUES	NONE
TABLES/SEATS	NONE

DIRECTIONS

The entrance is 18.6 km west of Carrathool Road and 20.2 km east of Glencoe Road

GPS -34.514175 145.233636

Mulberrygong has good access to the river at its boundaries. Good quality tracks allow 2WD access, but are 4WD when wet. Trailer boat launching using 4WD or remote launch is available at the downstream campsite. There are large areas of open, flat camping capable of supporting large groups in isolation. Shore based fishing is good around structure.

102. BURRABOGIE RESERVE

ACCESS ROADS	★★★
BOAT RAMP	★
CAMPING	★★★
SWIMMING	★
SHORE BASED FISHING	★★★★
TOILETS	NONE
SHADE	★★★★
BINS	NONE
BARBEQUES	NONE
TABLES/SEATS	NONE

DIRECTIONS

The entrance is 25.7 km west of Carrathool Road and 13.4 km east of Glencoe Road.

GPS -34.502860 145.159861

Burrabogie is an accessible reserve that offers three main camping areas. The main track forks 400 m from the gate with the right hand track leading to an open campsite (suitable for caravans) and excellent angling banks. The left hand track proceeds toward the downstream boundary of the reserve. A large, open campsite is available by taking the first track to the right. The downstream boundary is a secluded area where trailer boat launching is difficult, but possible using 4WD. Tracks are 2WD, but slippery when wet.

103. NULABOR RESERVE

ACCESS ROADS	★★★
BOAT RAMP	★★★★
CAMPING	★★★★
SWIMMING	★★★
SHORE BASED FISHING	★★★★
TOILETS	NONE
SHADE	★★★★
BINS	NONE
BARBEQUES	NONE
TABLES/SEATS	NONE

DIRECTIONS

The entrance is 13.7 km east of the Mid-Western Highway along the Murrumbidgee River Road and 29.5 km west of Carrathool Road.

GPS -34.460083 145.121453

Nulabor features an open, shady campsite with excellent swimming and shore based fishing and an easy trailer boat launch site. The main camping area is small, but could accommodate several groups. This campsite is located straight ahead along the track from the entrance. A track continues for several kilometres along the riverfront downstream accessing secondary campsites and boat launching locations. Good shore based fishing is found along the entire waterfront.

REGION OVERVIEW
MAP 13 - HAY

BALRANALD
MAUDE
MAP 13
HAY
UARDRY
CARRATHOOL
YARADDA / BENEREMBAH
DARLINGTON POINT
YANCO
NARRANDERA
GALORE
WAGGA WAGGA
CURRAWARNA
OURA
WANTABADGERY
GUNDAGAI

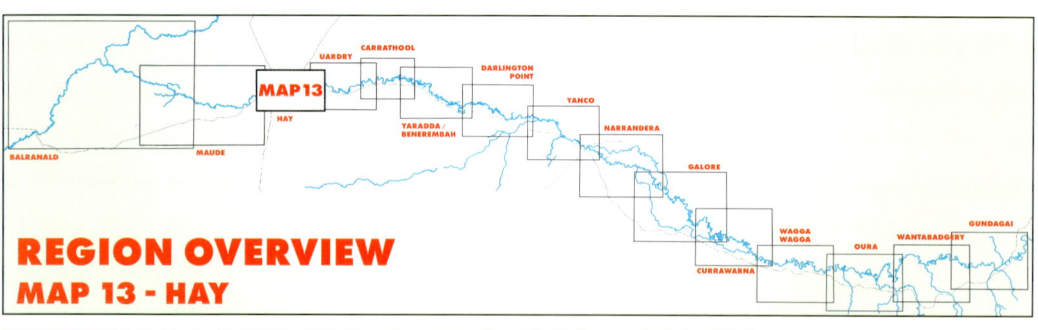

HAY TOWNSHIP
SOAPWORKS BEND
To Maude
Maude Road
Cadell Street
To Hay Weir
112
Moppett Street
Water Street
Lachlan Street
111
110
109
108
COBB HIGHWAY
Murray Street
MID WESTERN HIGHWAY
MURRUMBIDGEE VALLEY REGIONAL PARK (HAY)
Bourke Street
Bagot Street
107
STURT HIGHWAY
To Narrandera
To Balranald
SANDY POINT (HAY BOAT RAMP)
Shear Outback Museum
Roset Street
CEMETERY BEND
Old Common Road
BRANDON'S BEND
BUSHY BEND
To Deniliquin
0 0.4 0.8 1.2 1.6 2 Kilometres
ILLILAWA RESERVE
Yankee Crossing Road
SOAPWORKS BEND
CEMETERY BEND
MID WESTERN HIGHWAY
FOUR MILE RESERVE
HAY
106
105
To Maude
112
113
109
108
107
114
115
STURT HIGHWAY
ELI ELWAH RESERVE
To Balranald
Shear Outback Museum
BRANDON'S BEND
Old Common Road
MURRUMBIDGEE VALLEY REGIONAL PARK (WOOLOONDOOL)
MURRUMBIDGEE VALLEY REGIONAL PARK (HAY)
SIX MILE RESERVE
COBB HIGHWAY
To Deniliquin

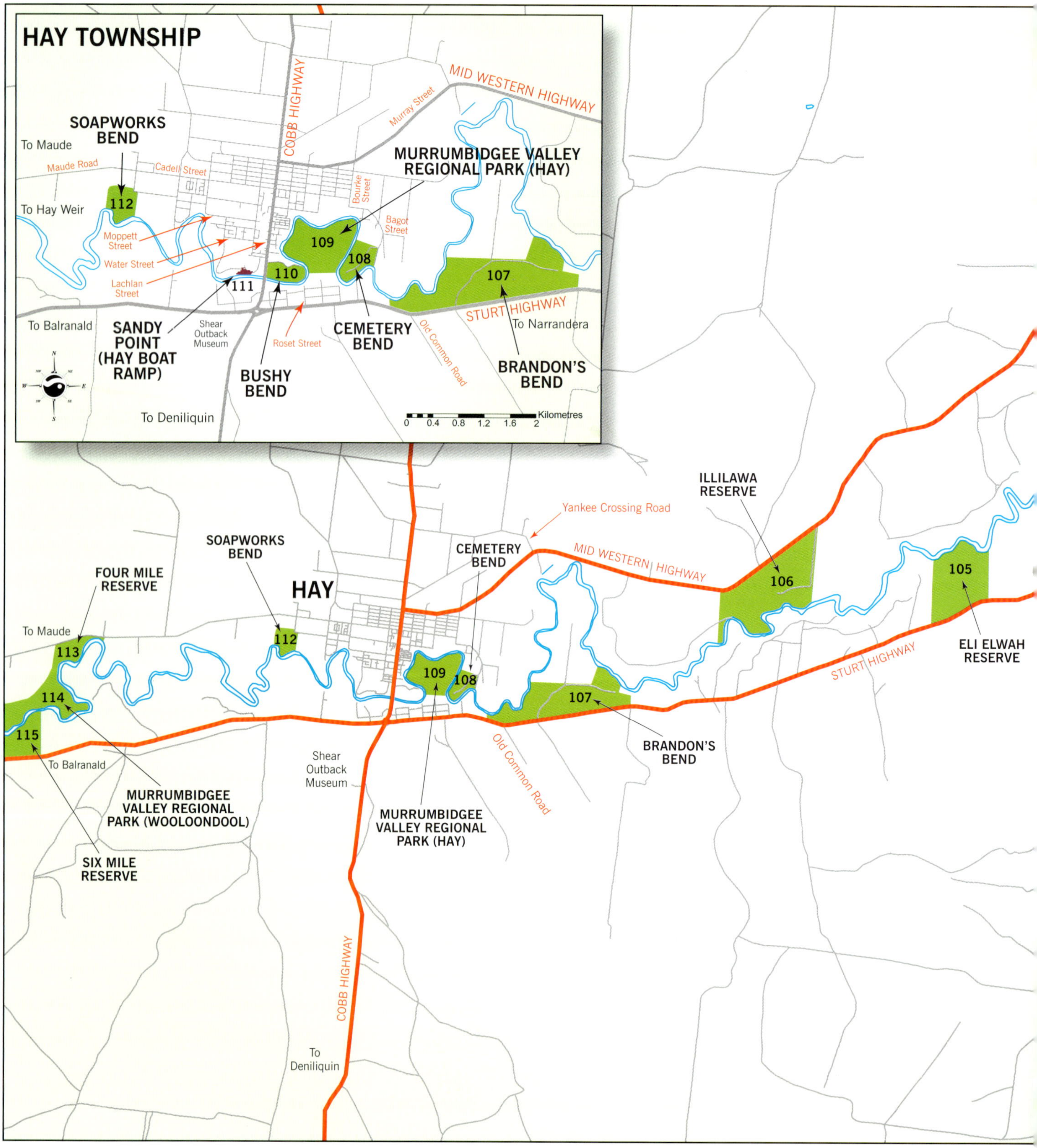

HAY REGION

Made famous internationally by Banjo Patterson's poem Hay, Hell and Booligal, the Hay region is typified by completely flat, open, treeless saltbush plains. Charles Sturt explored the region in his whaleboat in 1829/30 and was followed a decade later by squatters who set up large properties. The 'Illilawa' run, established in the 1840s, contained the land on which northern Hay is built whilst Hay South developed on land that was part of the 'Eli-Elwah' run and the Mungadingadal (now Mungadal) run was occupied by the Lang Brothers. An important river crossing existed on Mungadal where stock heading south to the Victorian markets or north to pasture would rest before fording the river. In World War II Hay was used as a POW and internment centre housing Jewish internees, Japanese internees, along with German and Italian POWs. After the war, Italian migrants arrived in Hay and established market gardens.

104. MERRIOLA RESERVE

DIRECTIONS

The entrance is 3.4 km east of the Mid-Western Highway along the Murrumbidgee River Road and 39.8 km west of Carrathool Road.

GPS -34.467971 145.016381

Merriola is a large area with a riverside track providing access in several locations. Cliffs at the upstream and downstream boundaries limit access to the river. The best campsite is located on a beach area, east of where the main track first meets the river (-34.476491 145.023691). This location has gently sloping banks that provide trailer boat launching using 4WD or remote-launch. Access roads are good with secondary tracks winding through the trees parallel to the river. These secondary tracks are slippery when wet. Shore based fishing is best around snags.

ACCESS ROADS	★★★
BOAT RAMP	★★★
CAMPING	★★★★
SWIMMING	★★★★
SHORE BASED FISHING	★★★★
TOILETS	NONE
SHADE	★★★★
BINS	NONE
BARBEQUES	★
TABLES/SEATS	NONE

105. ELI ELWAH RESERVE

ACCESS ROADS	★★★
BOAT RAMP	★★★
CAMPING	★★★★
SWIMMING	★★★
SHORE BASED FISHING	★★★★
TOILETS	★★
SHADE	★★★★
BINS	NONE
BARBEQUES	NONE
TABLES/SEATS	NONE

DIRECTIONS

The entrance is 5.3 km west of Glencoe Road and 9.0 km east of Old Common Road.

GPS -34.506314 144.963649

Eli Elwah has one main camping area under shady trees that offers a pit toilet. Trailer boat launching is available at this area using 4WD or remote launch. Secondary roads lead to more secluded campsites that are mostly situated on high banks. Angling is best downstream of the main campsite. The river is navigable and has excellent boat and shore based fishing.

106. ILLILAWA RESERVE

DIRECTIONS

The entrance is 5.9 km east of Bourke Street along the Mid-Western Highway and 7.6 km west of the Murrumbidgee River Road and Mid-Western Highway intersection (i.e. the Carrathool sign).

GPS -34.499304 144.916790

ACCESS ROADS	★★★★
BOAT RAMP	★★★
CAMPING	★★★★
SWIMMING	★★★★
SHORE BASED FISHING	★★★★
TOILETS	NONE
SHADE	★★★★★
BINS	★★★
BARBEQUES	NONE
TABLES/SEATS	NONE

Illilawa is a large reserve which offers many flat, open and shaded campsites suitable for caravans. Camp sites toward the eastern end of the reserve (track left from entrance) have gently sloping banks providing trailer boat launching using 4WD or remote launch. The western campsites (track right from entrance) offer better shore based fishing with steeper banks and more in-stream structure. Tracks are generally in good condition, but are slippery when wet. Swimming is excellent with gently sloping banks and low current providing ideal conditions.

107. BRANDON'S BEND

DIRECTIONS

The eastern entrance is 13.8 km west of Glencoe Road and 900 m east of Old Common Road. The western entrance is 200 m west of Old Common Road.

GPS -34.522752 144.865284

Brandon's Bend has numerous campsites and fishing locations. The waterfront is accessed using a track that parallels the water's edge. The reserve is a good location to fish upper reaches of the Hay weir pool. The tracks are 2WD when dry and 4WD when wet. There are two main entrances and a number of secondary tracks providing access to the reserve from the highway. The boat launch site (-34.520399 144.867314) is best accessed from the western entrance and is suitable for launching large trailer boats with 4WD or remote launch. The river is wide, still and deep providing excellent shore and boat based fishing.

ACCESS ROADS	★★★
BOAT RAMP	★★★
CAMPING	★★★
SWIMMING	★★
SHORE BASED FISHING	★★★★
TOILETS	NONE
SHADE	★★★
BINS	NONE
BARBEQUES	NONE
TABLES/SEATS	NONE

108. CEMETERY BEND

DIRECTIONS

Turn south from the Mid Western Highway (east of Hay township) into Bourke Street. Continue for 1.3 km, then turn right into Underwood Road. Veer right after 100 m to the reserve entrance.

GPS -34.512529 144.862984

ACCESS ROADS	★★★
BOAT RAMP	★★★
CAMPING	★★★
SWIMMING	★★★
SHORE BASED FISHING	★★★★
TOILETS	NONE
SHADE	★★★★
BINS	NONE
BARBEQUES	NONE
TABLES/SEATS	★★

The main tracks into this reserve are 2WD accessible. Secondary tracks along the waterfront are rough due to 4WD activity and impassable when wet. The upstream boundary (i.e. left track at entrance) offers easy trailer boat launching and excellent access to the river for shore based fishing. A second launch site is located toward the middle of the reserve. There are numerous campsites and shore based fishing is excellent. The slow, deep water creates ideal boat fishing.

109. MURRUMBIDGEE VALLEY REGIONAL PARK (HAY)

ACCESS ROADS	★★★★
BOAT RAMP	★★
CAMPING	★★★
SWIMMING	★★★
SHORE BASED FISHING	★★★★
TOILETS	NONE
SHADE	★★★★
BINS	NONE
BARBEQUES	NONE
TABLES/SEATS	NONE

DIRECTIONS

At 1.6 km west of Old Common Road (or 700 m east of Sturt Highway and Cobb Highway roundabout), turn into Roset Street. Proceed around the right hand bend and then turn immediately left onto the dirt track and continue behind the large water tank to the Park entrance.

GPS -34.519552 144.849976

Murrumbidgee Valley Regional Park (Hay) has well-groomed roads that circle the forest boundary. There are two main camping areas off the main track, both offering good angling. Trailer boat launching is possible (4WD only) at the campsite at the north western end of the Park (located by taking the left hand track at entrance). Swimming and shored based fishing are excellent at this site. The second campsite is located on the north east corner and is an excellent angling location.

110. BUSHY BEND

DIRECTIONS

Access the reserve at the northern end of the bridge over the Murrumbidgee River (opposite the skate park).

GPS -34.515477 144.843289

ACCESS ROADS	★★★★
BOAT RAMP	NONE
CAMPING	NONE
SWIMMING	★★
SHORE BASED FISHING	★★★★★
TOILETS	NONE
SHADE	★★★★
BINS	★★★★★
BARBEQUES	NONE
TABLES/SEATS	★★★★★

Bushy Bend is a reserve in the heart of Hay. The Bidgee Riverside Trail meanders through this neat, shady reserve with several picnic areas, many with tables. Shore based fishing is excellent around the bridge and at the various campsites. The one-way track loops around the reserve and is 2WD (slippery in wet weather). Bushy Bend is an ideal angling location and a scenic place for a picnic. No boat launching is available.

111. SANDY POINT (HAY BOAT RAMP)

ACCESS ROADS	★★★★
BOAT RAMP	★★★★★
CAMPING	★★★★
SWIMMING	★★★★★
SHORE BASED FISHING	★★★★
TOILETS	★★★★★
SHADE	★★★★★
BINS	★★★★★
BARBEQUES	★★★★★
TABLES / SEATS	★★★★★

DIRECTIONS

There are two entrances to Sandy Point. The first is accessed from Lachlan Street by turning into Brunker Street and then left again into the reserve. The second entrance is accessed from Water Street.

GPS -34.515212 144.842403

Sandy Point showcases the river precinct with maintained grounds, toilet facilities, barbeques, a concrete boat ramp and shaded tables suitable for large groups. Sandy Point is an ideal rest stop for travellers offering excellent swimming, amenities and fishing opportunities. Sandy Point provides access to the start of the Bidgee Riverside Trail. Camping is permitted in the designated area, which is suitable for caravans.

112. SOAPWORKS BEND

ACCESS ROADS	★★★★
BOAT RAMP	★★★★★
CAMPING	★★★★
SWIMMING	★★
SHORE BASED FISHING	★★★★★
TOILETS	★★
SHADE	★★★★
BINS	NONE
BARBEQUES	NONE
TABLES / SEATS	NONE

DIRECTIONS

The entrance is 10.9 km east of the Hay Weir sign and 2.2 km west of Lachlan Street along Cadell Street (i.e. the Maude Road).

GPS -34.503204 144.821499

Soapworks Bend is a picturesque, well-maintained camping and picnic area close to Hay township. It offers a concrete boat ramp, and open, flat camp sites under a shaded canopy. The tracks are well-groomed and suited to 2WD (4WD when wet). This is an excellent location for camping, travel breaks or to launch your boat and access the excellent fishing in the weir pool. Shore based fishing is excellent.

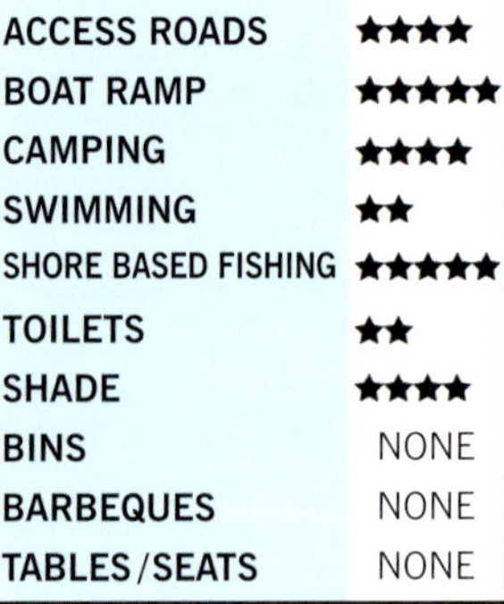

113. FOUR MILE RESERVE

DIRECTIONS

The entrance is 6.6 km east of the Hay Weir sign and 6.5 km west of Lachlan Street along Cadell Street (i.e. the Maude Road).

GPS -34.506179 144.773509

Four Mile Reserve features a concrete ramp enabling launching of all sized trailer boats. Adjacent to the boat ramp there are several open, flat campsites. The waterfront has easy access providing excellent shore based fishing opportunities. The weir pool has excellent boat based fishing and navigable water.

ACCESS ROADS	★★★★
BOAT RAMP	★★★★★
CAMPING	★★★
SWIMMING	★★
SHORE BASED FISHING	★★★★
TOILETS	NONE
SHADE	★★★★
BINS	NONE
BARBEQUES	NONE
TABLES/SEATS	NONE

114. MURRUMBIDGEE VALLEY REGIONAL PARK (WOOLOONDOOL)

DIRECTIONS

The access track is 6.4 km east of the Hay Weir sign and 6.7 km west of Lachlan Street along Cadell Street (i.e. the Maude Road) on the western side of the irrigation channel. Proceed for 600 m to the Regional Park entrance gate.

GPS -34.506781 144.771037

Murrumbidgee Valley Regional Park (Wooloondool) has numerous open, flat camp sites. The main track leads directly to the downstream boundary campsite. While this site could accommodate large groups, boat launching is difficult due to the steep bank. More secluded campsites and excellent trailer boat launching are available toward the middle of the Park using the left track from the entrance. The tracks are 2WD, but 4WD when wet. Shore based fishing is excellent along the entire waterfront with deep water and drowned timber providing ideal fish habitat.

ACCESS ROADS	★★★
BOAT RAMP	★★★
CAMPING	★★★★★
SWIMMING	★★★
SHORE BASED FISHING	★★★★★
TOILETS	NONE
SHADE	★★★★
BINS	NONE
BARBEQUES	NONE
TABLES/SEATS	NONE

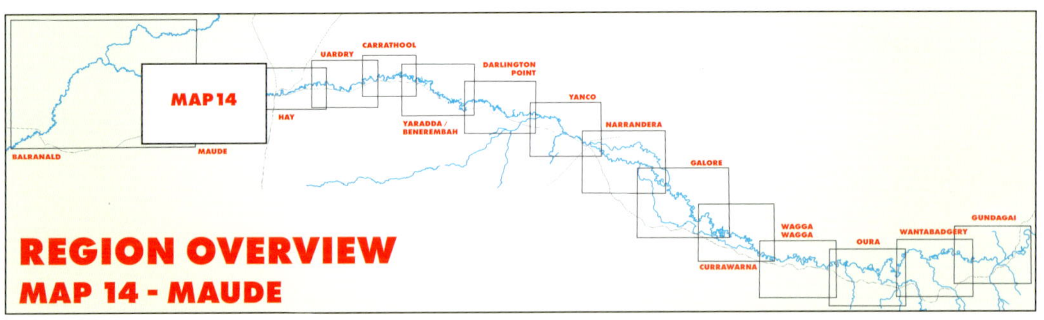

MAP 14
BALRANALD
MAUDE
HAY
UARDRY
CARRATHOOL
YARADDA / BENEREMBAH
DARLINGTON POINT
YANCO
NARRANDERA
GALORE
CURRAWARNA
WAGGA WAGGA
OURA
WANTABADGERY
GUNDAGAI
REGION OVERVIEW
MAP 14 - MAUDE

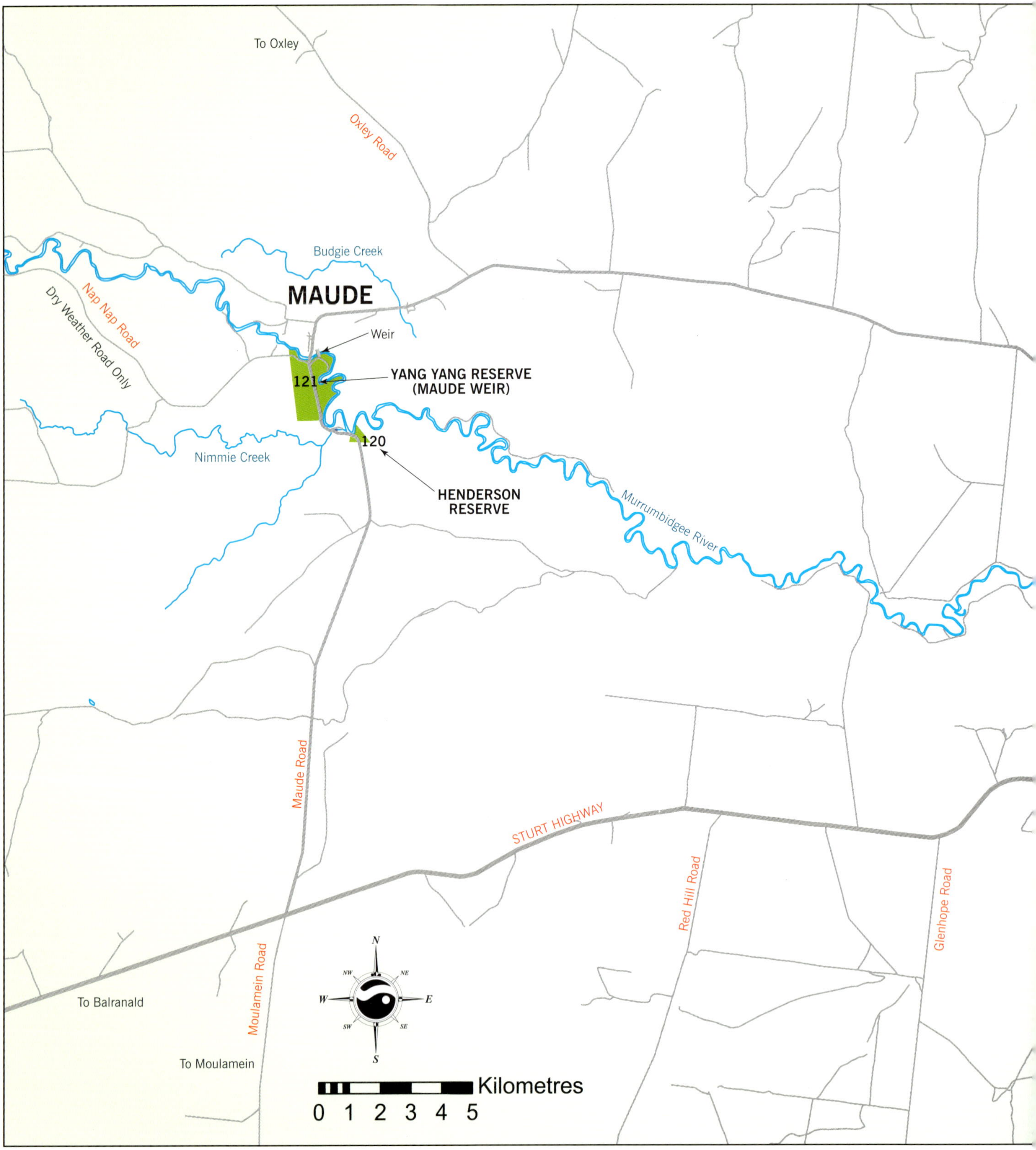

To Oxley
Oxley Road
Budgie Creek
MAUDE
Nap Nap Road
Dry Weather Road Only
Weir
121
YANG YANG RESERVE
(MAUDE WEIR)
120
HENDERSON
RESERVE
Nimmie Creek
Murrumbidgee River
Maude Road
STURT HIGHWAY
Red Hill Road
Glenhope Road
Moulamein Road
To Balranald
To Moulamein
N
NE
E
SE
S
SW
W
NW
Kilometres
0 1 2 3 4 5

MAUDE REGION

Maude started its existence as a hotel beside a river ford in the late 1850s. Riverboats provided an important link between Maude and the outside world, travelling upstream along the Murrumbidgee and downstream to the Murray. The dominant feature of this region is the flat plains. Even though Maude lies 1530 km from the mouth of the Murray, it's only 76 m above sea level (essentially, the land rises 5 cm per kilometre). Aside from the plains, Maude features a weir, which took two years to build from 1937 to 1939, providing work for 60 men in the depression years. The weir was built to regulate the Murrumbidgee and to divert water for irrigation purposes. The weir and surrounds are ideal locations for fishing, camping, a picnic or barbecue lunch.

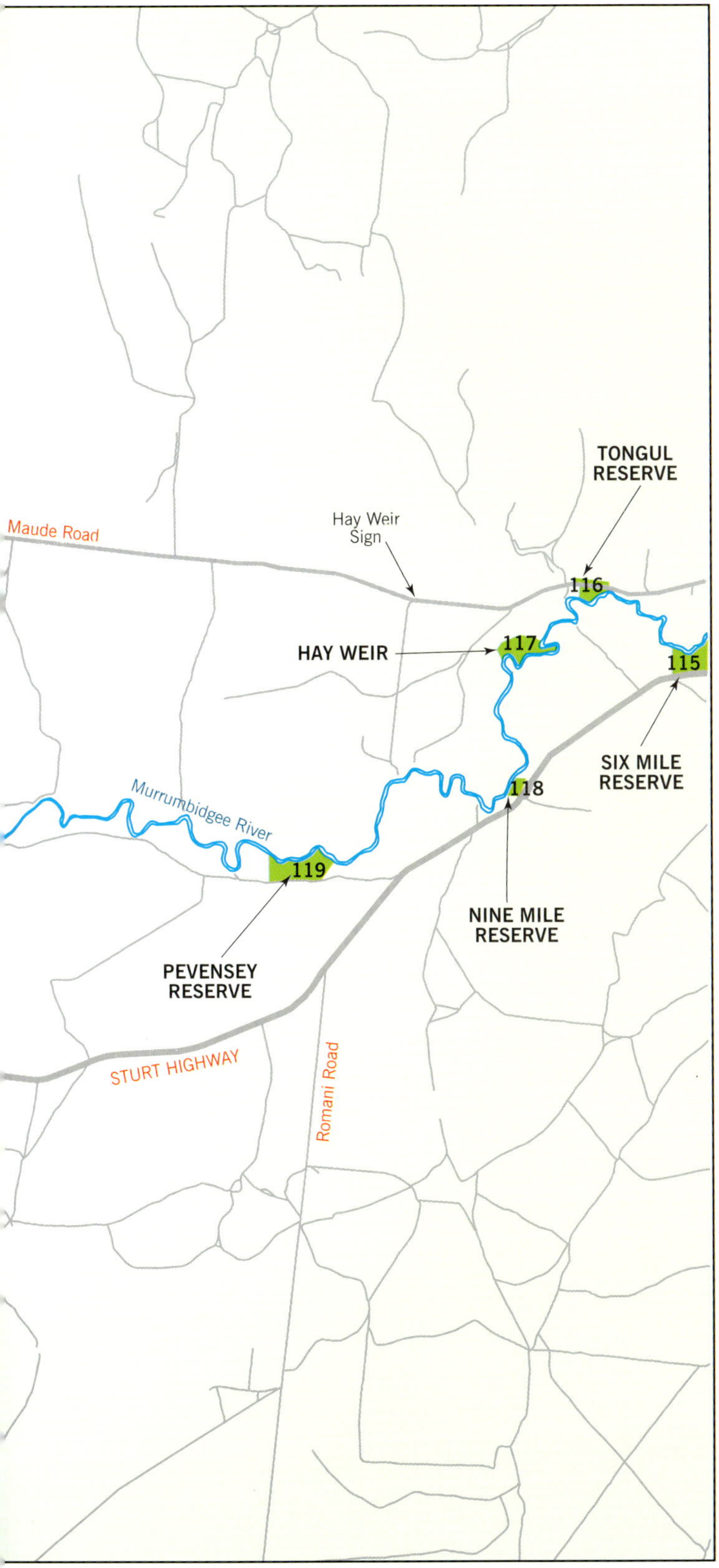

115. SIX MILE RESERVE

DIRECTIONS

The access road is 8.1 km west of the Sturt Highway and Cobb Highway roundabout and 11.1 km east of Romani Road. Turn north from the Highway along the dirt track, after 50 m, veer right off the main track and proceed to the river. Secondary tracks exist accessing other campsites.

GPS -34.527712 144.755231

Six Mile Reserve offers excellent camping, fishing and easy access to the backed up waters of Hay Weir. There are several campsites with better locations at the eastern boundary where the river fills the lagoon. Trailer boats are easily launched at this site with 4WD or remote launch. Shore based fishing is good, however, boating allows access to a greater variety of habitat, from deep channels, to shallow lagoons and densely timbered backwaters. Tracks are slippery when wet.

ACCESS ROADS	★★★★
BOAT RAMP	★★★
CAMPING	★★★★
SWIMMING	★★
SHORE BASED FISHING	★★★
TOILETS	NONE
SHADE	★★★
BINS	NONE
BARBEQUES	NONE
TABLES/SEATS	NONE

116. TONGUL RESERVE

DIRECTIONS

The entrance is 2.8 km east of the Hay Weir sign and 10.2 km west of Lachlan Street along Cadell Street (i.e. the Maude Road).

GPS -34.509343 144.736041

ACCESS ROADS	★★★★
BOAT RAMP	★★★
CAMPING	★★★★★
SWIMMING	★★
SHORE BASED FISHING	★★★★★
TOILETS	NONE
SHADE	★★★★
BINS	NONE
BARBEQUES	NONE
TABLES/SEATS	NONE

Tongul Reserve offers a reasonable dirt boat ramp and open campsites under large red gums. It's an ideal location to camp and access the backed up waters of Hay Weir. The deep, still water and drowned timber create ideal fish habitat and accordingly shore and boat based fishing are excellent. There are several entrances to the reserve with all tracks leading to the main camp area and boat launch. The tracks are 2WD, but slippery when wet.

117. HAY WEIR

ACCESS ROADS	★★★★
BOAT RAMP	★
CAMPING	★★★
SWIMMING	★
SHORE BASED FISHING	★★★★
TOILETS	NONE
SHADE	★★★
BINS	NONE
BARBEQUES	NONE
TABLES/SEATS	NONE

DIRECTIONS

The entrance road (Weir Road) is 33.8 km east of the Oxley Road and Maude Road intersection and 12.2 km west of Lachlan Street along Cadell Street (i.e. the Maude Road). Travel 2 km along Weir Road to the entrance.

GPS -34.512838 144.705005

The Hay Weir precinct provides access to the river above and below the weir. Trailer boat launching above the weir is available from the dirt ramp adjacent to the yellow buoys. The area above the weir has several flat, open campsites offering excellent shore based fishing. Road access above the weir is 2WD. The boat ramp at Fisherman's Plateau (below the weir) offers a difficult 4WD launch. Below the weir the tracks are 2WD when dry and 4WD in wet weather. Campsites below the weir are limited, but shore based angling is excellent.

118. NINE MILE RESERVE

DIRECTIONS

The access road is 13.0 km west along the Sturt Highway from the Sturt and Cobb Highway roundabout and 6.2 km east of Romani Road.

GPS -34.552535 144.712928

ACCESS ROADS	★★★
BOAT RAMP	★
CAMPING	★★★
SWIMMING	★★
SHORE BASED FISHING	★★★
TOILETS	NONE
SHADE	★★★★
BINS	NONE
BARBEQUES	NONE
TABLES/SEATS	NONE

Nine Mile Reserve provides access to the Murrumbidgee River below Hay Weir. The reserve offers several campsites, but river access is limited due to steep banks. Trailer boat launching is restricted, but there is a difficult 4WD remote launch at the downstream boundary. This reserve is ideal for shore based fishing with excellent fish habitat. Camping is good with adequate shade and flat, open areas.

119. PEVENSEY RESERVE

ACCESS ROADS	★★★
BOAT RAMP	★
CAMPING	★★★
SWIMMING	★★★★
SHORE BASED FISHING	★★★
TOILETS	NONE
SHADE	★★★★
BINS	NONE
BARBEQUES	NONE
TABLES/SEATS	NONE

DIRECTIONS

Turn into the unsealed public access road at the 'Pevensey' property sign, 16.6 km west of the Sturt and Cobb Highway roundabout at Hay and 2.6 km east of Romani Road. Continue over two cattle grids and immediately turn right into the reserve. Do not proceed past the third cattle grid as this is private property.

GPS -34.568652 144.680979

Pevensey Reserve has several small campsites either on top of high banks or on a beach. The tracks are 2WD when dry, but 4WD when wet. These tracks are unsuitable for caravans. Boat launching is difficult across the beach using 4WD remote launch. The beach is an excellent location for swimming. Note that the reserve boundary is unfenced and care should be taken not to stray onto private land. Drive only on the tracks and respect the landowner's property.

120. HENDERSON RESERVE

ACCESS ROADS	★★★
BOAT RAMP	★★★
CAMPING	★★★
SWIMMING	★
SHORE BASED FISHING	★★★★
TOILETS	NONE
SHADE	★★★
BINS	NONE
BARBEQUES	NONE
TABLES/SEATS	NONE

DIRECTIONS

The entrance is 15.7 km from the Sturt Highway along the Maude Road. From Maude, the entrance is 700 m past Nimmie Creek.

GPS -34.503236 144.316707

Henderson Reserve is a small well-shaded area with limited camp sites. Trailer boat launching using 4WD or remote launch is available using the gully. Access roads are 2WD (4WD when wet) and suitable for caravans. The river is easily accessible and provides excellent shore and boat based fishing opportunities.

121. YANG YANG RESERVE (MAUDE WEIR)

DIRECTIONS

Yang Yang Reserve includes areas above and below Maude Weir. Above the weir, there are three reserve entrances. The main entrance is 550 m from Nap Nap Road and 1.8 km from Nimmie Creek. Other entrances are immediately south of the bridge and 700 m from Nimmie Creek over the grid. The track to the downstream boat launch and camp is located 600 m along Nap Nap Road.

GPS -34.486441 144.302151

ACCESS ROADS	★★★
BOAT RAMP	★★★
CAMPING	★★★★
SWIMMING	★
SHORE BASED FISHING	★★★★
TOILETS	NONE
SHADE	★★★★
BINS	NONE
BARBEQUES	NONE
TABLES/SEATS	NONE

There are numerous campsites upstream of Maude Weir within Yang Yang Reserve. Many of these are located at the ends of secondary tracks. The main track is 2WD, but 4WD when wet. Most campsites are open, well shaded and have easy access to the river. Trailer boat launching above the weir (4WD or remote launch) is best at an area 200 m from the main entrance (veer right at the T-intersection to the boat ramp area). Note that when the weir pool level is high, boats may be launched at many other locations. Boat fishing is excellent with deep, easily navigable water and sunken timber providing good fish habitat. Yang Yang Reserve continues downstream of Maude Weir (on the southern shore) with several camp sites suitable for caravans and a boat launching area (4WD or remote launch) at -34.477213 144.294636. Shore based fishing below the weir is excellent.

MAP 15
BALRANALD
MAUDE
HAY
UARDRY
CARRATHOOL
YARADDA / BENEREMBAH
DARLINGTON POINT
YANCO
NARRANDERA
GALORE
WAGGA WAGGA
CURRAWARNA
OURA
WANTABADGERY
GUNDAGAI
REGION OVERVIEW
MAP 15 - BALRANALD

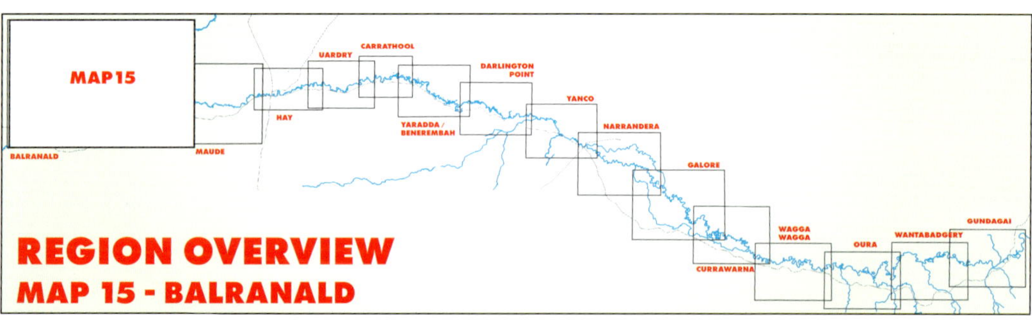

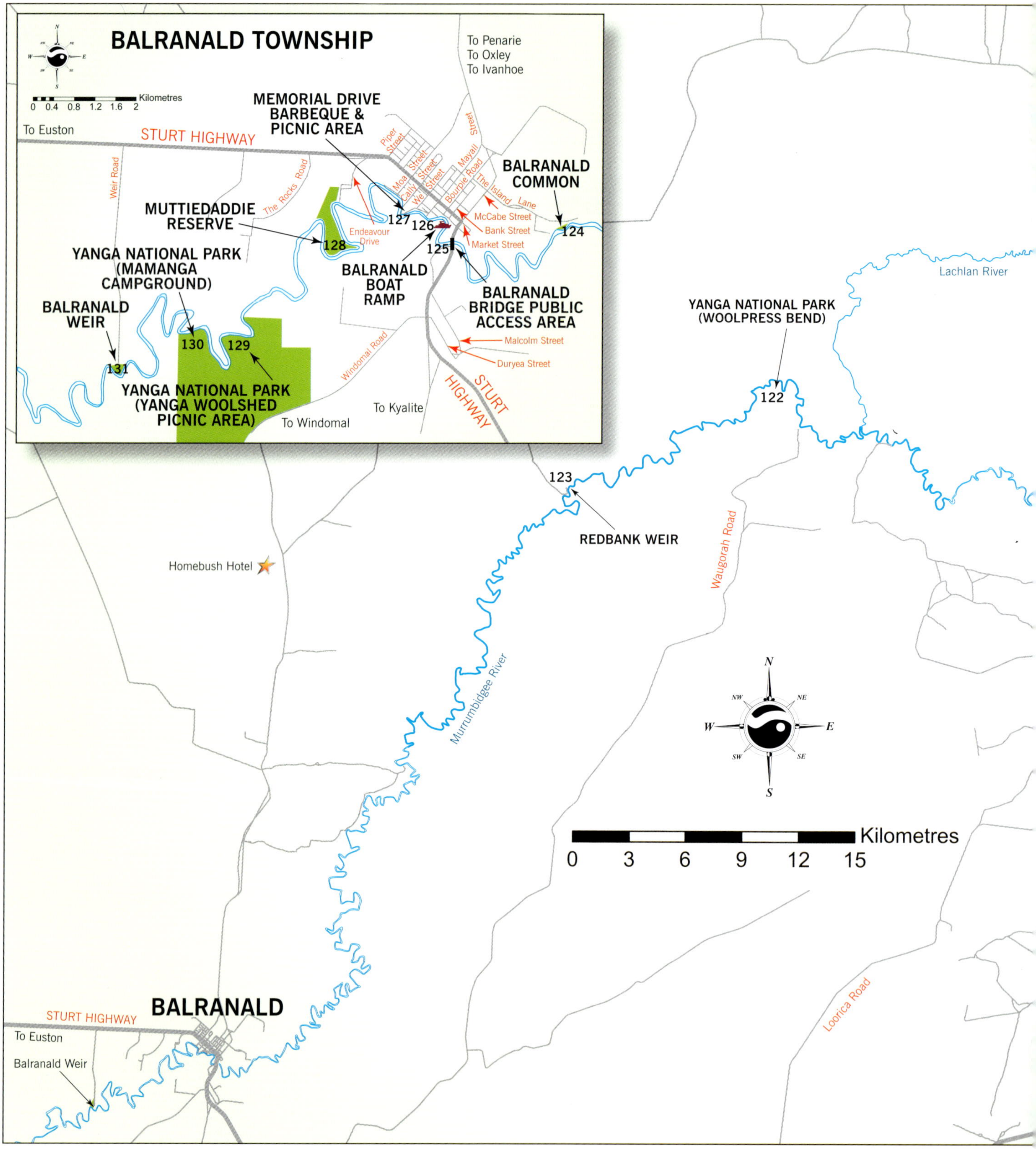

BALRANALD TOWNSHIP
Kilometres
0 0.4 0.8 1.2 1.6 2
To Penarie
To Oxley
To Ivanhoe
To Euston
STURT HIGHWAY
MEMORIAL DRIVE BARBEQUE & PICNIC AREA
BALRANALD COMMON
Weir Road
The Rocks Road
Piper Street
Moa Street
Caily Street
We Street
Bourke Road
Mayall Street
The Island Lane
McCabe Street
Bank Street
Market Street
Endeavour Drive
MUTTIEDADDIE RESERVE
YANGA NATIONAL PARK (MAMANGA CAMPGROUND)
BALRANALD WEIR
BALRANALD BOAT RAMP
BALRANALD BRIDGE PUBLIC ACCESS AREA
Malcolm Street
Duryea Street
Windomal Road
YANGA NATIONAL PARK (YANGA WOOLSHED PICNIC AREA)
To Windomal
To Kyalite
STURT HIGHWAY
124
125
126
127
128
129
130
131
Lachlan River
YANGA NATIONAL PARK (WOOLPRESS BEND)
122
123
REDBANK WEIR
Waugorah Road
Homebush Hotel
Murrumbidgee River
N
NE
E
SE
S
SW
W
NW
Kilometres
0 3 6 9 12 15
STURT HIGHWAY
BALRANALD
To Euston
Balranald Weir
Loorica Road

BALRANALD REGION

The Balranald region is largely a flat saltbush and Mallee plain. The township of Balranald is a service centre for the surrounding irrigation district, which has expanded from conventional agriculture to viticulture, horticulture and tourism. Considered the oldest settlement on the lower Murrumbidgee, the area was occupied by the Wemba-Wemba people, who called the area 'Nap Nap'. The explorers, John Oxley (1817), Charles Sturt (1830), Thomas Mitchell (1836) and Burke and Wills (1860) all passed through this region in their efforts to open up Australia's interior. The region offers two weirs, a low level weir at Balranald and Redbank Weir (58 km north-east), which has barbecues and picnic tables, public toilets and a well-maintained grassed area overlooking the river.

122. YANGA NATIONAL PARK (WOOLPRESS BEND)

ACCESS ROADS	★★★
BOAT RAMP	★★★
CAMPING	★★★★
SWIMMING	★
SHORE BASED FISHING	★★★★
TOILETS	★★★★
SHADE	★★★★
BINS	NONE
BARBEQUES	NONE
TABLES/SEATS	★★★★

DIRECTIONS

Turn north from the Sturt Highway onto Waugorah Road. Continue for 44.3 km (roads are unsealed after 29.8 km). Keep left on Waugorah Road at the intersection with the old, red fridge mailboxes. Continue for 5.0 km (crossing the bridge over Waugorah Creek), then keep right on Waugorah trail to the entrance gate. Turn left at the entrance gate (past the information shelter) and continue 3.8 km to the intersection that leads to each campground. Keens Camp and Sandy Bend Camp are to the left. Woolpress Bend Picnic Area and Cooba Bend Camp are to the right.

GPS -34.373899 143.895975

Woolpress Bend campground has four distinct areas, Keens Camp, Sandy Bend Camp, Cooba Bend Camp and Woolpress Bend Picnic Area (day use only). Each site can accommodate large groups and provides toilets, tables/seats and easy access to the backed up water of the Redbank Weir pool. Trailer boat launching is available at each site using 4WD or remote launch. Access tracks are 2WD and suitable for caravans, but 4WD when wet. Bookings for each camp are required. Contact Yanga National Park office to make a booking.

123. REDBANK WEIR

ACCESS ROADS	★★★★
BOAT RAMP	NONE
CAMPING	NONE
SWIMMING	★
SHORE BASED FISHING	★★★★★
TOILETS	★★★★
SHADE	★★★★
BINS	★★★
BARBEQUES	★★★
TABLES/SEATS	★★★

DIRECTIONS

In Balranald, turn north from Market Street (Sturt Highway) onto Mayall Street (the Ivanhoe Road). Continue for 26.2 km until you reach the Homebush Hotel. Approximately 300 m past the Homebush Hotel turn right into Oxley Road. Follow this road for 13 km, then turn right at the Redbank Weir sign. Follow the unsealed Redbank Weir road for 12 km to the picnic ground.

GPS -34.318643 143.701201

Redbank Weir has well-groomed facilities and is ideal for a riverside picnic overlooking the weir structure. Camping is not permitted downstream or upstream of the weir. The public access road into the weir is 2WD, but slippery when wet. Note that the land adjacent to the access road is private property with no public access.

124. BALRANALD COMMON

ACCESS ROADS	★★★
BOAT RAMP	★★
CAMPING	★★★
SWIMMING	★★
SHORE BASED FISHING	★★★★
TOILETS	NONE
SHADE	★★★★
BINS	NONE
BARBEQUES	NONE
TABLES/SEATS	NONE

DIRECTIONS

From the eastern end of Market Street (Sturt Highway) turn left into McCabe Street. Proceed for 700 m and turn right onto The Island Lane. Travel straight for 1.4 km (past the cemetery and the house) then veer right off the lane into the reserve.

GPS -34.644977 143.587527

Balranald Common has several campsites linked by numerous tracks. The access roads are 2WD, but slippery when wet. Shore based fishing is excellent with good fish holding structure and deep water. Boat launching (via 4WD, or remote launch) is possible at the upstream boundary. This reserve is ideal for shore based angling with easy access to deep, snag filled water in a number of locations.

125. BALRANALD BRIDGE PUBLIC ACCESS AREA

ACCESS ROADS	★★★★
BOAT RAMP	★
CAMPING	NONE
SWIMMING	★
SHORE BASED FISHING	★★★★
TOILETS	NONE
SHADE	★★★★
BINS	NONE
BARBEQUES	NONE
TABLES/SEATS	★★★★

DIRECTIONS

Turn west from the Sturt Highway into the unnamed entrance, 100 m south of the Murrumbidgee River Bridge at Balranald.

GPS -34.649905 143.565783

Balranald Bridge has several open, flat sites, linked by a riverside track. The access roads are 2WD, but slippery when wet. Shore based fishing is good with fish holding structure and deep water along the waterfront. Boat launching (via 4WD remote launch) is possible underneath the bridge. Camping is not permitted.

126. BALRANALD BOAT RAMP

ACCESS ROADS	★★★★★
BOAT RAMP	★★★★★
CAMPING	NONE
SWIMMING	★
SHORE BASED FISHING	★★★★
TOILETS	NONE
SHADE	★★★★
BINS	★★★★
BARBEQUES	NONE
TABLES/SEATS	NONE

DIRECTIONS

The entrance lane is located on the eastern side of the Sturt Highway at the intersection of Court and McCabe Streets (beside the War Memorial). Continue under bridge to boat ramp.

GPS -34.645922 143.567466

Balranald Boat Ramp is an excellent concrete facility offering sealed accessed roads and a floating pontoon. The facilities allow boat launching in all weather conditions and water levels. Shore based fishing opportunities are available but limited in space. Camping is not permitted.

127. MEMORIAL DRIVE BARBEQUE AND PICNIC AREA

ACCESS ROADS	★★★★
BOAT RAMP	★★★★
CAMPING	NONE
SWIMMING	★★
SHORE BASED FISHING	★★★★
TOILETS	NONE
SHADE	★★★★★
BINS	★★★★★
BARBEQUES	★★★★
TABLES/SEATS	★★★★★

DIRECTIONS

Turn south from Market Street (Sturt Highway) onto Cally Street. Memorial Drive Barbeque and Picnic Area is directly ahead. Secondary access is also available from We Street.

GPS -34.641380 143.556426

Memorial Drive is a well-maintained public area with manicured lawns, an electric barbeque and numerous tables and seats. Camping isn't permitted, however there is a day parking area and a concrete boat ramp allowing boats of all sizes to be launched. Shore based fishing is excellent in both the reserve and along the walking track which extends upstream from the picnic area. This is an ideal location to launch a trailer boat to fish the slow, deep waters of the weir pool.

128. MUTTIEDADDIE RESERVE

ACCESS ROADS	★★★
BOAT RAMP	★★
CAMPING	★★★
SWIMMING	★★
SHORE BASED FISHING	★★★★
TOILETS	NONE
SHADE	★★★
BINS	NONE
BARBEQUES	NONE
TABLES/SEATS	NONE

DIRECTIONS

Turn south onto Endeavour Drive from the Sturt Highway. Proceed for 700 m and turn right (before church) into a small gravel laneway. Turn left at the T intersection, then travel a further 100 m and turn right through gate to access reserve.

GPS -34.639242 143.542441

Muttiedaddie is a large reserve with numerous secondary trails stemming from the main track (i.e the middle track 50 m from gate), many of which lead to campsites along the extensive river frontage. The tracks are 2WD, but 4WD when wet. Shore based fishing is excellent with deep, slow water created by Balranald Weir, abundant submerged snags and easy access to the water. Trailer boat launching using 4WD or remote launch is available toward the end of the main track in the south east corner of the reserve at -34.648935 143.544333.

129. YANGA NATIONAL PARK (YANGA WOOLSHED PICNIC AREA)

DIRECTIONS

Turn south from the Sturt Highway on Windomal Road. Continue for 3.0 km, then turn right at the sign to Yanga Woolshed. Continue along the track to the left of the sheds for 1.6 km to the picnic area.

GPS -34.675370 143.531997

ACCESS ROADS	★★★★
BOAT RAMP	NONE
CAMPING	NONE
SWIMMING	★★
SHORE BASED FISHING	★★★★
TOILETS	★★★★
SHADE	★★★★
BINS	★★★★
BARBEQUES	★★★★★
TABLES/SEATS	★★★★★

Yanga Woolshed Picnic Area is a scenic spot beside the Murrumbidgee River. The picnic area provides facilities including a large covered area with several picnic tables and gas barbecues. The access roads are 2WD and 4WD when wet. Shore based fishing is good with easy access to the waterfront. The picnic area is day use only.

ACCESS ROADS	★★★
BOAT RAMP	★★
CAMPING	★★★★
SWIMMING	★★
SHORE BASED FISHING	★★★★
TOILETS	★★★★
SHADE	★★★★
BINS	NONE
BARBEQUES	NONE
TABLES/SEATS	★★★

130. YANGA NATIONAL PARK (MAMANGA CAMPGROUND)

DIRECTIONS

Turn south from the Sturt Highway on Windomal Road. Continue for 4.1 km, then turn right at the sign to Mamanga Campground. Continue along the track for 1 km to the camping areas.

GPS -34.680078 143.520795

Mamanga campground is a large, secluded area with separate sections for tent camping and another open area suitable for caravans. The access roads are 2WD (slippery when wet). Shored based fishing is good with ample access to the shoreline. Boat launching is available using 4WD or remote launch.

131. BALRANALD WEIR

DIRECTIONS

Proceed west from Balranald along the Sturt Highway. Turn south into Weir Road 3.6 km west from The Rocks Road. (Note: the road leading to the weir is 4 km long).

GPS -34.629954 143.497139

ACCESS ROADS	★★★★
BOAT RAMP	NONE
CAMPING	★★★
SWIMMING	NONE
SHORE BASED FISHING	★★★★
TOILETS	NONE
SHADE	★★
BINS	NONE
BARBEQUES	★★
TABLES/SEATS	★★★

Balranald Weir regulates water before it enters the Murray River approximately 100 km downstream near the small township of Boundary Bend. River access is available above and below the weir for shore based fishing in either the slow, deep water of the weir pool, or the shallow, fast-running water of the tailrace. No boat launching is available above or below the weir. Access tracks are 2WD when dry (slippery when wet) and suitable for caravans. There are several open, flat areas for camping.

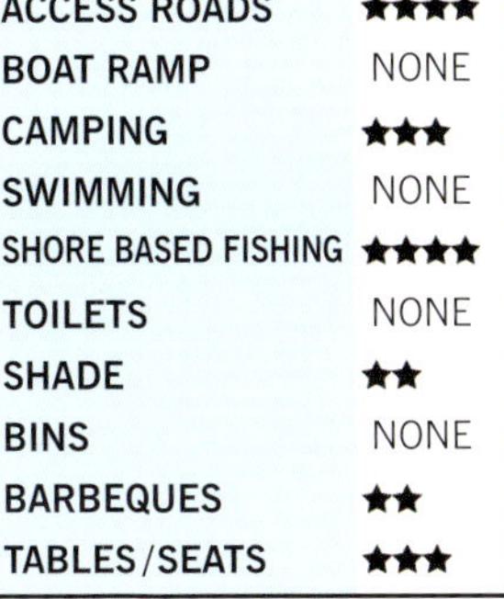

CHAPTER 8
APPENDICES

APPENDIX 1
GUIDE TO USING GPS COORDINATES

GPS stands for Global Positioning System, which is a network of satellites that continuously transmit coded information making it possible to precisely identify locations on earth by measuring distance from the satellites. The GPS locations listed in this guide use latitude and longitude formatted as degree decimal. In order to navigate to the GPS locations listed in this guide you will need to have your GPS receiver set up with the following coordinate system settings:

Coordinate system:	Latitude/Longitude (degree decimal)
Map Datum:	GDA 94
North Reference:	True North

APPENDIX 2
VISITOR INFORMATION CENTRES

GUNDAGAI VISITOR INFORMATION CENTRE
249 Sheridan Street
Gundagai NSW 2722
Phone (02) 6944 0250
Email: info@visitgundagai.com.au

WAGGA WAGGA VISITORS CENTRE
183 Tarcutta Street
Wagga Wagga NSW 2650
Phone 1300 100 122
Email: visitors@wagga.nsw.gov.au

LEETON VISITORS INFORMATION CENTRE
10 Yanco Avenue
Leeton NSW 2705
Phone (02) 6953 6481
Email: enquiries@leetontourism.com.au

NSW DEPARTMENT OF PRIMARY INDUSTRIES
Narrandera Fisheries Centre
70 Buckingbong Road
Narrandera NSW 2700
Phone (02) 6958 8200

NARRANDERA VISITOR INFORMATION CENTRE
26 Cadell Street (Newell Highway)
Narrandera NSW 2700
Phone (02) 6959 5545
Email: tourist.centre@narrandera.nsw.gov.au

HAY VISITOR INFORMATION CENTRE
407 Moppett Street
Hay NSW 2711
Phone: (02) 6993 4045
Email: visithay@hay.nsw.gov.au

BALRANALD VISITOR INFORMATION CENTRE
83 Market St, Balranald NSW 2715
Phone (03) 5020 1599
Email: infocentrestaff@balranald.nsw.gov.au

APPENDIX 3

ENJOYING CROWN RESERVES

The Crown Reserve System is the oldest and most diverse system of land management in NSW with land reserved for public purposes since colonial times. The reserve system is used for a wide range of public purposes including environmental and heritage protection, recreation and sport, open space, community halls and special events.

Camping in Crown reserves is permitted, with fires allowed at times of year when total fire bans are not in place. Rubbish bins are generally not available (with the exception of some major reserves in townships) and users should remove all rubbish. Swimming is a popular pastime within riverside Crown reserves and care should be taken with shallow water, fast currents and submerged objects. The erection of rope swings and the like is neither encouraged nor tolerated.

For information about usage of Crown reserves in your region contact your local NSW Crown Lands office.

NSW CROWN LAND OFFICES

General enquiries
437 Hunter Street, Newcastle NSW 2300. Phone: 1300 886 235. Email: cl.enquiries@crownland.nsw.gov.au

WAGGA WAGGA CROWN LANDS
Cnr Johnston & Tarcutta Streets
Wagga Wagga NSW 2650

GRIFFITH CROWN LANDS
Farm 217, Murray Road, Hanwood
Griffith NSW 2680

HAY CROWN LANDS
126 Lachlan Street
PO Box 182 Hay NSW 2711

APPENDIX 4

ENJOYING TRAVELLING STOCK RESERVES

The Travelling Stock Reserve (TSR) network was established more than 150 years ago to allow the movement of livestock to and from markets. Many of these routes are believed to have followed pathways used traditionally by Indigenous people to travel across country and many adjoin rivers. Local Land Services are responsible for the care, control and management of TSR land.

TSRs can be used by graziers during times of drought, bushfire and flood as supplementary grazing areas or for apiary sites. Permits are required from the Local Land Services for these activities. TSRs can also be used by members of the public for recreation between sunrise and sunset and other uses such as conservation.

LOCAL LAND SERVICES OFFICES

REGIONAL OFFICE
Building 24, Darnell Smith Drive
Charles Sturt University
Wagga Wagga NSW 2678
Phone: 1300 795 299 or (02) 6923 6300
Email: admin.riverina@lls.nsw.gov.au

GUNDAGAI
87 Sheridan Street
Gundagai NSW 2722
Phone: (02) 6940 6900

GRIFFITH
200 Murray Road
Hanwood NSW 2680
Phone: (02) 6960 1300

NARRANDERA
8 Bolton Street
Narrandera NSW 2700
Phone: (02) 6958 1800

BALRANALD
82 Market Street
Balranald NSW 2715
Phone: (03) 5020 1691

HAY
56 Lachlan Street
Hay NSW 2711
Phone: (02) 6990 1300

APPENDIX 5
ENJOYING STATE FORESTS

Normal road rules apply to driving in state forests. Vehicles must be registered and drivers/riders appropriately licensed. Care should be taken in state forests as log trucks, bushwalkers, cyclists and animals may also be using the same roads. In addition, heavy equipment such as excavators, bulldozers and graders can be encountered at any time.

Drivers should keep to formed roads and fire trails. Creating new tracks can damage vegetation and lead to soil erosion and pollution of waterways. During wet weather it is best to avoid using forest roads to prevent rutting and track erosion. State forests can be very large and help can be a long way away.

Ensure that your vehicle is mechanically sound and carry a first aid kit, fire extinguisher, food and drinking water, fuel and recovery equipment for your vehicle.

During total fire ban periods open fires are not permitted anywhere in a state forest. At other times ensure your campfire is in a properly cleared area, or preferably in a formed fireplace. Firewood collection is permitted in some state forest areas outside the fire danger period, however a permit is required. Keep camp sites clean and take your rubbish home with you. Please follow all road signage, and respect road closures due to timber harvesting.

STATE FOREST OFFICES

Forestry Corporation Head Office
121-131 Oratava Ave
West Pennant NSW 2125
Phone: 1300 655 687
Email: info@fcnsw.com.au

APPENDIX 6
ENJOYING NATIONAL PARKS

Dotted across the landscape between Narrandera and Balranald are a series of river red gum forests that make up the Murrumbidgee Valley National Park and the Murrumbidgee Valley Regional Park. These parks are close to Narrandera, Yanco, Leeton, Hay and Balranald (Yanga National Park). Camping is free with no booking requirements for sites. Small campfires are allowed in the river red gum forests outside of the solid fuel ban period. A solid fuel fire ban applies between 31 October and 31 March each year. Park management may vary this if local conditions change. If you do have a small campfire, make sure you completely extinguish all fires before leaving an area or going to bed. A small amount of glowing embers can start a bushfire. Dogs are only allowed in regional parks, not national parks, so check your location beforehand.

NATIONAL PARKS OFFICES

NATIONAL PARKS CONTACT CENTRE
Phone: 1300 072 757
Email: parks.info@environment.nsw.gov.au

GRIFFITH NPWS
200 Yambil Street
Griffith NSW 2680
Phone (02) 6966 8100
Email: npws.riverina@environment.nsw.gov.au

YANGA NATIONAL PARK
38773 Sturt Highway
Yanga NSW 2711
Phone: (03) 5020 1764
Email: npws.lowerdarling@environment.nsw.gov.au

No matter where you are, ARB has you covered.

VICTORIA

ARB STORES

Head Office
ARB Kilsyth
42-44 Garden Street
Kilsyth VIC 3137
Tel: (03) 9761 6622

ARB Bairnsdale
623 Princes Highway
Bairnsdale VIC 3875
Tel: (03) 5152 1226

ARB Ballarat
891 Latrobe Street
Delacombe VIC 3356
Tel: (03) 5336 4605

ARB Bendigo
17-21 Phillips Drive
Kangaroo Flat VIC 3555
Tel: (03) 5445 7100

ARB Brighton
793 Nepean Highway
Bentleigh VIC 3204
Tel: (03) 9557 1888

ARB Dandenong
4A/6 Lonsdale Street
Dandenong VIC 3175
Tel: (03) 9793 0002

ARB Echuca
89A Ogilvie Avenue
Echuca VIC 3564
Tel: (03) 5840 2600

ARB Geelong
304 Thompson Road
North Geelong VIC 3215
Tel: (03) 5272 2611

ARB Hoppers Crossing
73-79 Old Geelong Road
Hoppers Crossing VIC 3029
Tel: (03) 9749 5905

ARB Keilor Park
34 Commercial Place
Keilor East VIC 3033
Tel: (03) 9331 7333

ARB Pakenham
20 Commercial Drive
Pakenham VIC 3810
Tel: (03) 5940 5500

ARB Shepparton
180 Benalla Road
Shepparton VIC 3630
Tel: (03) 5822 1877

ARB Somerton
798 Cooper Street
Somerton VIC 3074
Tel: (03) 9460 9988

ARB Traralgon
351 Princes Highway
Traralgon East VIC 3844
Tel: (03) 5174 9190

ARB Warragul
10 Howitt Street
Warragul VIC 3820
Tel: (03) 5623 5599

ARB STOCKISTS

Gippsland 4WD Centre
Lot 7 Princes Highway
Traralgon VIC 3844
Tel: (03) 5174 1560

Highcountry Parts & 4×4
201 Mt Buller Road
Mansfield VIC 3722
Tel: (03) 5779 1900

Horsham Off Road
72 McPherson Road
Horsham VIC 3400
Tel: (03) 5381 1766

Mildura 4WD Accessories
55 Seventh Street
East Mildura VIC 3500
Tel: (03) 5021 3213

Myrtleford Tyre & Battery
73 Myrtle Street
Myrtleford VIC 3737
Tel: (03) 5752 1175

Outback 4WD
174 Canterbury Road
Bayswater VIC 3153
Tel: (03) 9720 6226

Sale 4WD Centre
21-23 Union Street
Sale VIC 3850
Tel: (03) 5144 7990

SG Offroad Leongatha
2 Tilson Court
Leongatha VIC 3953
Tel: (03) 5662 5554

SG Offroad Wonthaggi
136 McKenzie Street
Wonthaggi VIC 3995
Tel: (03) 5672 5899

South Eastern 4WD Centre
182 Centre Road
Narre Warren VIC 3805
Tel: (03) 8786 5090

Swan Hill Off Road
1 Nyah Road
Swan Hill VIC 3585
Tel: (03) 5032 2700

Wangaratta 4WD Centre
205 Tone Road
Wangaratta VIC 3677
Tel: (03) 5722 2979

Warrnambool Offroad
1117 Raglan Parade
Warrnambool VIC 3280
Tel: (03) 5561 4354

Yarra Valley 4WD
35 Maroondah Highway
Healesville VIC 3777
Tel: (03) 5962 3124

WESTERN AUSTRALIA

ARB STORES

ARB Bunbury
2/12 George Street
Bunbury WA 6230
Tel: (08) 9721 2099

ARB Canning Vale
77 Bannister Road
Canning Vale WA 6155
Tel: (08) 9455 4366

ARB Geraldton
78 North West
Coastal Hwy
Geraldton WA 6530
Tel: (08) 9921 8077

ARB Mandurah
69 Gordon Road
Mandurah WA 6210
Tel: (08) 9583 3200

ARB Osborne Park
66 Collingwood Street
Osborne Park WA 6017
Tel: (08) 9244 3553

ARB South Hedland
2 Hamilton Road
South Hedland WA 6722
Tel: (08) 9160 4900

ARB Wangara
11 Buckingham Drive
Wangara WA 6065
Tel: (08) 9409 5764

ARB Welshpool
143 Welshpool Road
Welshpool WA 6106
Tel: (08) 9358 3688

ARB STOCKISTS

Action 4WD
19 Gillam Drive
Kelmscott WA 6111
Tel: (08) 9390 3011

Adventure 4×4
3 Crocker St
Rockingham WA 6168
Tel: (08) 9529 2229

Albany 4WD & Camping Centre
6 Minna Street
Albany WA 6331
Tel: (08) 6819 7777

All 4×4 Services
63 Strelly Street
Busselton WA 6280
Tel: (08) 9754 8588

Avon 4 Wheel Drive Centre
20 Peel Terrace
Northam WA 6401
Tel: (08) 9622 5818

Derby 4×4 and Marine
Lot 920 Wells Street
Derby WA 6728
Tel: (08) 9193 1919

Falcon Auto Parts & Accessories
Unit 17 651-669
Old Coast Rd
Falcon WA 6210
Tel: (08) 9534 6722

Kununurra 4WD Spares
21 Konkerberry Dr
Kununurra WA 6743
Tel: (08) 9169 1150

Make Tracks
44 Elgee Road
Midland WA 6056
Tel: (08) 9374 0777

Minshull Mechanical Repairs
96 Guy Street
Broome WA 6725
Tel: (08) 9192 5326

North West 4×4
2 Coghlan Street
Broome WA 6725
Tel: (08) 9194 5600

Off Road Equipment Myaree
61 McCoy Street
Myaree WA 6154
Tel: (08) 9317 4900

Pilbara Motor Group
7 Crane Circle
Karratha WA 6714
Tel: (08) 9144 6500

Pilbara Motor Group - Newman
18 Pardoo Street
Newman WA 6753
Tel: (08) 9154 3600

Southern Suspension & 4WD Centre
53 Norseman Road
Esperance WA 6450
Tel: (08) 9072 0917

Traction 4WD
179 Boulder Road
South Kalgoorlie WA 6430

TASMANIA

ARB STORES

ARB Burnie
1A Edwardes Street
South Burnie TAS 7320
Tel: (03) 6431 4494

ARB Hobart
5-9 Florence Street
Moonah TAS 7009
Tel: (03) 6232 2333

ARB Launceston
48 Holbrook Street
Invermay TAS 7248
Tel: (03) 6331 4190

ARB STOCKISTS

North West Off Road
24 Kelcey Tier Road
Spreyton TAS 7310
Tel: (03) 6427 3266

SOUTH AUSTRALIA

ARB STORES

ARB Edwardstown
957 South Road
Melrose Park SA 5039
Tel: (08) 8293 3225

ARB Elizabeth
27 Elizabeth Way
Elizabeth SA 5112
Tel: (08) 8252 1599

ARB Morphett Vale
181-183 Main South Road
Morphett Vale SA 5162
Tel: (08) 8186 6101

ARB Regency Park
606-608 South Road
Regency Park SA 5010
Tel: (08) 8244 5001

ARB STOCKISTS

Adelaide Off Road
65-67 Nelson Street
Stepney SA 5069
Tel: (08) 8363 5999

Allin Towbars
175 Richmond Road
Richmond SA 5033
Tel: (08) 8352 5155

Drop Bear 4×4 & Leisure
6B Augusta Highway
Port Augusta SA 5700
Tel: (08) 8642 2322

Clare Valley 4×4
273 Main North Road
Clare SA 5453
Tel: (08) 8842 3113

Copper Triangle
2-4 Graves Street
Kadina SA 5554
Tel: (08) 8821 2402

Goeverywhere 4×4
599 North East Road
Gilles Plains SA 5086
Tel: (08) 8369 0999

Hoop's Auto & 4WD Centre
232 Renmark Avenue
Renmark SA 5341
Tel: (08) 8586 5519

Jacksons 4×4 Accessories
61 Chris Collins Court
Murray Bridge SA 5253
Tel: (08) 8532 2550

LMG Performance
11276 Augusta Highway
Warnertown SA 5540
Tel: (08) 8634 3118

Mount Barker 4×4 Centre
1 Mount Barker Road
Mount Barker SA 5250
Tel: (08) 8391 4391

Port Lincoln 4WD
28-30 Mortlock Terrace
Port Lincoln SA 5606
Tel: (08) 8682 2424

Trident Tyre Centre
16 McDonnell Street
Naracoorte SA 5271
Tel: (08) 8762 3744

Trident Tyre Services
16 Bay Road
Mt Gambier SA 5290
Tel: (08) 8725 7799

Victor Harbor 4WD Centre
20-24 Adelaide Road
Victor Harbor SA 5211
Tel: (08) 8552 2543

NORTHERN TERRITORY

ARB STORES

ARB Alice Springs
30 Stuart Highway
Alice Springs NT 0870
Tel: (08) 8953 0572

ARB Darwin
892 Stuart Highway
Pinelands NT 0828
Tel: (08) 8947 2262

ARB STOCKISTS

Gove Motors
Arnhem Road
Nhulunbuy NT 0880
Tel: (08) 8987 1911

L&S Offroad
16 Jessop Crs
Berrimah NT 0828
Tel: (08) 8947 4771

Palmerston 4WD Spares - 4WD Repair Center
33 Georgina Crescent
Palmerston NT 0830
Tel: (08) 8932 3233

RJ Motors Katherine
1833 Stuart Highway
Katherine NT 0850
Tel: (08) 8972 2269

ACT

ARB STORES

ARB Fyshwick
188-190 Gladstone Street
Fyshwick ACT 2609
Tel: (02) 6280 7475